EUREKA!
2G

Success in Science

Carol Chapman
Rob Musker
Daniel Nicholson
Moira Sheehan

Heinemann

Heinemann Educational Publishers
Halley Court, Jordan Hill, Oxford OX2 8EJ
Part of Harcourt Limited
Heinemann is the registered trademark of Harcourt Education Limited

First published 2001

ISBN 0 435 57626 7

05 04
10 9 8 7 6 5

Edited by Ruth Holmes

Designed and typeset by Ken Vail Graphic Design, Cambridge

Original illustration © Heinemann Educational Publishers 2001

Illustrated by Graham-Cameron Illustration (Harriet Buckley, Sarah Wimperis), SGA
(Stephen Sweet), Nick Hawken, Margaret Jones, B L Kearley Ltd. (Shirley Bellwood),
David Lock, Richard Morris, Sylvie Poggio Artists Agency (Tim Davies).

Printed and bound in Spain by Edelvives

Picture research by Jennifer Johnson

Acknowledgments
The authors and publishers would like to thank the following for permission to use
copyright material:
extract p2, Dispatch, spring 1996 volume VII, No 1; **extract p18,** Daily Mail
13/3/99, **extract p106,** Birmingham Evening Mail 8/12/98; **text and illustrations
p112,** The Hungary Caterpillar by Eric Carle 1970.

The publishers have made every effort to trace the copyright holders, but if they have
inadvertently overlooked any, they will be pleased to make the necessary
arrangements at the first opportunity.

For photograph acknowledgements, please see page 154.

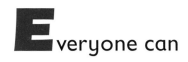

Everyone can

Understand science by

Reading this book, be

Enthralled, become

Knowledgeable and

Achieve success…

…with EUREKA!

Eureka!
I've got it.

SYRACVSE BATH HOVSE

WASHIUM ET GOIUM

PROPERTY OF S·B·H

Welcome to *Eureka! Success in Science*

This is the second of three books designed to help you learn all the science ideas you need during Key Stage 3. We hope you'll enjoy the books as well as learning a lot from them.

These two pages will help you get the most out of the book so it's worth spending a couple of minutes reading them!

This book has nine units which each cover a different topic. The units have three types of pages:

Setting the scene

Each unit starts with a double-page spread which reminds you of what you know already about the topic. They tell you other interesting things, such as the place of science in everyday life and the history of some science inventions and ideas.

Learn about

► Energy

Most of the double-page spreads in a unit introduce and explain new ideas about the topic. They start with a list of these so that you can see what you are going to learn about.

Think about

► Fair tests
► Variables

Each unit has a double-page spread called Think about. You will work in pairs or small groups and discuss your answers to the questions. These pages will help you understand how scientists work and how ideas about science develop.

On the pages there are these symbols:

(a) Make a list of foods that give you a lot of energy.

Quick questions scattered through the pages help you check your knowledge and understanding of the ideas as you go along.

Questions

The questions at the end of the spread help you check you understand all the important ideas.

For your notes

These list the important ideas from the spread to help you learn, write notes and revise.

This shows there is a practical activity which your teacher may give you. These will help you plan and carry out investigations into ideas about science and collect and analyse results and evaluate your work.

 This shows there is an ICT activity which your teacher may give you. You will use computers to collect results from datalogging experiments, or work with spreadsheets and databases, or get useful information from CD-ROMS or the Internet.

 This shows there is a writing activity which your teacher may give you to help you write about the science you learn.

 This shows there is a discussion activity which your teacher may give you. You will share your ideas about science with others in a discussion.

At the back of the book:

 All the important scientific words in the text appear in **bold** type. They are listed with their meanings in the Glossary at the back of the book. Look there to remind yourself what they mean.

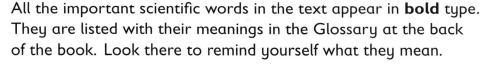 There is an index at the very back of the book, where you can find out which pages cover a particular topic.

Activities to check your learning

Your teacher may give you these activities:

Lift-off!
When you start a unit, this short exercise reminds you what you already know about a topic.

Unit map
You can use this to think about what you already know about a topic. You can also use it to revise a topic before a test or exam.

Quiz
You can use the quiz at the end of each unit to see what you are good at and what you might need to revise.

Revision 1
You can use the revision sheets to revise a part of a unit which you aren't so good at.

End of unit test
This helps you and your teacher check what you learned during the unit, and measures your progress and success.

Contents

T indicates Think about spread

Acid accident

Runaway Train Derails, Spills Sulfuric Acid down Mountainside

A runaway train derailed in the pre-dawn hours in Leadville, Colorado, killing two railroad employees and injuring a third. The February accident sent a river of sulfuric acid down a snowy mountainside and across a highway.

Why is sulfuric acid dangerous?

Concentrated sulfuric acid is **corrosive**. This means that it eats away most of the materials it touches, including human flesh! All corrosive substances have a warning label. These labels are used by the emergency services to help them decide how to manage an accident.

Dozens of drivers and rescue workers sought treatment at nearby medical facilities for exposure to fumes, with symptoms such as burning eyes, shortness of breath and nausea. Sulfuric acid is a corrosive acid that is highly poisonous by inhalation and causes severe burns in contact with skin tissue. Vapours are irritating to the eyes and throat.

The acid-tainted snow was collected and removed from the mountain.

a Make a list of the possible effects of sulfuric acid on the body.

b How do you think the snowy and icy weather helped make the acid spill less dangerous?

A solution

An **acid** is a solution of a particular kind of solid or gas in water. An acid that does not contain much water is a **concentrated** acid. An acid that contains quite a lot of water is called a **dilute** acid. In the Leadville accident, the snow melted and diluted the acid a little. Very dilute sulfuric acid is not corrosive.

c What do you think the fire service would do if a similar accident happened in this country during the summer?

Toxic means poisonous. Sulfuric acid is not labelled toxic.

d Read the newspaper extracts again. What word is better than 'poisonous' to describe sulfuric acid?

TOXIC poisonous

Useful acids

Sulfuric acid is a useful acid. For example, it is used in car batteries. You need to handle it carefully to avoid burning holes in your clothes or your skin.

We use products that contain acids every day, and not all of them are dangerous. Many acids are not corrosive – they do not burn or eat things away. Acids are less corrosive when you dilute them with water.

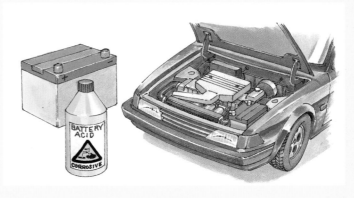

Acids in foods

Vinegar contains ethanoic acid.

Look at the photos. Many of the foods we eat contain acids. Some acids have very long names, but the word 'acid' is part of the name.

Your stomach also has acid in it. Too much stomach acid gives you indigestion. You can take tablets to treat the indigestion.

e Look at the pictures of foods. Make a list of all the acids you can see that are found in foods or drinks.

lactic acid   ascorbic acid, which is vitamin C

tannic acid

citric acid

Questions

1. Look at the word wall very carefully. It might remind you of some of the things you know about acids from talking to people, watching television or reading newspapers.

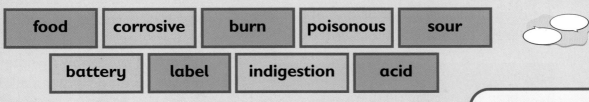

| food | corrosive | burn | poisonous | sour |

| battery | label | indigestion | acid |

Copy these sentences. Try using the words to complete them.

a Acid in food can give it a _____ taste.
b Some acids are _____ and _____.
c Too much stomach acid gives you _____.

Try to make some sentences of your own.
You will be surprised how much you already know about acids!

Did you know?

Rhubarb stalks are safe to eat, but the leaves contain poisonous oxalic acid. This puts animals off eating them!

Acids, bases and alkalis

Acids

Some acids are in foods. They have a sour taste. Other acids may be **corrosive**, **toxic**, **harmful** or **irritant**. They have a hazard warning label.

(a) Look at the hazard warning labels. Which hazard do you think is the least dangerous?

Bases and alkalis

Look at the photo showing substances found in the kitchen or bathroom. They all contain **bases**. A base is the opposite of an acid – it cancels out acidity.

Some bases dissolve in water. We call these **alkalis**. Like acids, many alkalis are corrosive, poisonous, harmful or irritant.

(b) What is the difference between an alkali and a base?

Safety first

The acids in food taste sour, but you must never taste a substance to find out whether it is an acid. You would know if you had spilled a corrosive acid on yourself as it would burn, whereas an alkali would feel soapy. However, you must never touch a substance to find out if it is an alkali. Many acids and alkalis are dangerous because they are corrosive.

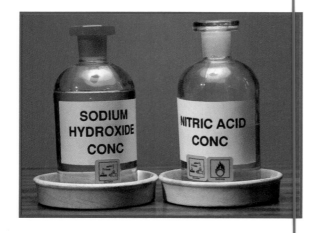

Learn about

- Acids, bases and alkalis
- Indicators

CORROSIVE
may destroy living tissues on contact

TOXIC
poisonous

HARMFUL
may have health risk if breathed in, taken internally or absorbed through skin

IRRITANT
non-corrosive substance which can cause red or blistered skin

Indicators

Using your senses is not a safe way of finding out whether a solution is acidic or alkaline. The best way is to use an **indicator**. An indicator is a coloured substance that shows whether a solution is an acid or an alkali. You can make an indicator using colours from flowers, fruits and vegetables. When an indicator is mixed with an acid or alkali, it changes colour.

(c) Find the word for a substance that changes colour when it is mixed with an acid or alkali.

Using litmus

Litmus is an indicator made from lichens. We use it in laboratories to find out whether solutions are acidic, alkaline or **neutral**. A neutral solution is neither acidic nor alkaline. Pure water is neutral.

- Litmus paper comes in small strips.
- You can use blue litmus paper or red litmus paper.
- To test a solution, dip a glass rod into it.
- Touch the litmus paper with the glass rod.

Acids turn blue litmus paper red. Alkalis turn red litmus paper blue. Both blue and red litmus paper stay the same colour with neutral solutions.

d What colour do you think blue litmus paper would turn in vinegar?

e What colour do you think red litmus paper would turn in soapy water?

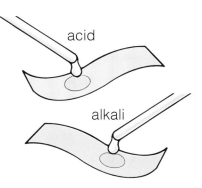

acid

alkali

> **Did you know?**
>
> Red cabbage acts as an indicator. It turns bright red in acid, and blue in alkali.

> **Did you know?**
>
> Your skin is slightly acidic, but soap is alkaline. Some skin cleansers and shampoos are slightly acidic, like the skin.

Questions

1. Copy and complete these sentences by choosing from the words below.

> acids   alkalis   litmus   plants
> substances   water

  a Indicators are coloured _____.
  b Many of them are made from _____.
  c An example of an indicator is _____.

2. a What colour does blue litmus turn in acid?
  b What colour does red litmus turn in alkali?
  c What colour is red litmus in a neutral solution?

3. a Draw hazard labels for:
    i corrosive   **ii** harmful   **iii** irritant.
  b Which label would you see on an acidic solution that burns the skin?

4. What safety precautions should you take when using acids in the laboratory?

> **For your notes**
>
> **Acids** can taste sour. Acids may be corrosive, poisonous, harmful or irritant.
>
> **Bases** are the opposites of acids. They cancel out acidity.
>
> An **alkali** is a soluble base. Alkalis can feel soapy. Alkalis may be corrosive, poisonous, harmful or irritant.
>
> A **neutral** solution is neither acidic nor alkaline.
>
> **Indicators** turn different colours with acidic, alkaline and neutral solutions.

Universal indicator

Litmus is very useful for telling whether a substance is acidic or alkaline, but it does not tell you how strong or weak it is or how dangerous it is. **Universal indicator** is another indicator made from plants. Because it is a mixture of indicators it can produce a range of colours. It will show a different colour for different strengths of acidic or alkaline solutions.

- Universal indicator comes in liquid or paper form.
- To use universal indicator liquid, add two drops to the solution you want to test.
- To use universal indicator paper, dip a glass rod into the solution. Touch the indicator paper with the glass rod.
- Compare the colour with the chart.

(a) When might universal indicator be more useful than litmus?

(b) Why does universal indicator give a range of colours?

The pH scale

Some acidic solutions are strongly acidic, and others are weakly acidic. The same is true for alkaline solutions. We use pH numbers to measure the strength of the acidity or alkalinity. (Remember to write it with a small 'p' and capital 'H'.) A neutral solution has pH 7. Acidic solutions have a pH less than 7. The lower the pH, the stronger the acidity. Look at the **pH scale** at the top of the next page. Hydrochloric acid is strongly acidic, with pH 1. Vinegar is more weakly acidic, with pH 3–4.

Alkaline solutions have a pH greater than 7. Sodium hydroxide solution is strongly alkaline, with pH 14. Ammonia is more weakly alkaline, with pH 11.

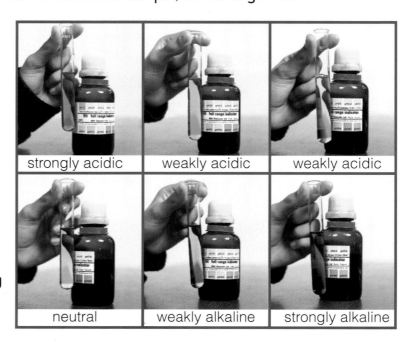

| strongly acidic | weakly acidic | weakly acidic |
| neutral | weakly alkaline | strongly alkaline |

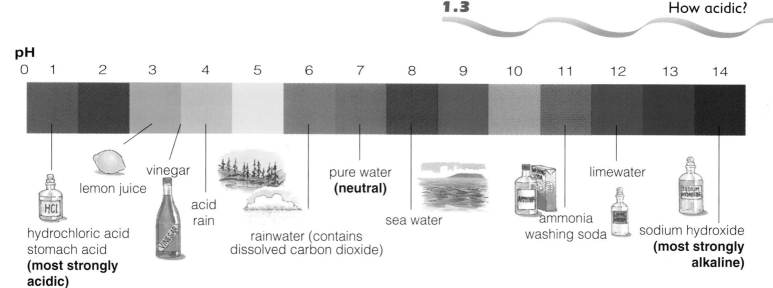

pH

0 1 2 3 4 5 6 7 8 9 10 11 12 13 14

lemon juice

vinegar

acid rain

rainwater (contains dissolved carbon dioxide)

pure water **(neutral)**

sea water

ammonia washing soda

limewater

sodium hydroxide **(most strongly alkaline)**

hydrochloric acid stomach acid **(most strongly acidic)**

Solutions of acids and alkalis can be **concentrated** or **dilute**. If you add water to a concentrated solution of an acid, it becomes more dilute.

c What is the difference between a concentrated acid and a dilute acid?

d What does the pH number tell us?

e Which word describes a substance with pH 7?

Questions

1. Look very carefully at the pH chart above. Copy the table below and complete it. The first line has been done for you.

Liquid	Colour with universal indicator	pH	Description
Indigestion medicine		9	Weakly alkaline
Tea			
Salt water			
Rainwater			
Soap			
Lemon juice			

2. Universal indicator paper turns blue with floor cleaner. What is the pH of floor cleaner?

3. Apple juice has pH 3. What colour will universal indicator turn with apple juice?

For your notes

An acidic solution may be strongly or weakly acidic. An alkaline solution may be strongly or weakly alkaline.

A **concentrated** acid or alkali becomes more **dilute** if you add water.

Universal indicator turns different colours with different strengths of acidity and alkalinity.

The **pH scale** is used to measure the strengths of acidic and alkaline solutions.

Water is neutral, so it has pH 7.

Cancelling out acidity

Putting them together

We say that a base is the opposite of an acid, because if you add a base to an acid you take away its acidity and make a new substance.

(a) What do you think happens if you mix a base with vinegar?

If you add vinegar to the base sodium hydrogencarbonate, you will see bubbles. The vinegar, which is an acid, is used up. We say that a chemical reaction has taken place. You cannot get the vinegar or the sodium hydrogencarbonate back.

When an acid reacts with a base, the chemical reaction that takes place is called **neutralisation**.

(b) How do we know that neutralisation is a chemical reaction?

Acid indigestion

Your stomach makes hydrochloric acid which helps to digest your food. The stomach has a special layer which stops the acid corroding your insides! Sometimes the stomach produces too much acid and you might get acid indigestion. This happens because you have eaten too much, not because you have eaten acidic food.

(c) What causes acid indigestion?

(d) How do you think acid indigestion can be treated?

Indigestion remedies are sometimes called 'antacids' or 'anti-acids'. They have alkalis or bases in them to neutralise the stomach acid. Before all these medicines were available, people just used to take a spoonful of sodium hydrogencarbonate in a glass of water. It was cheap and it worked!

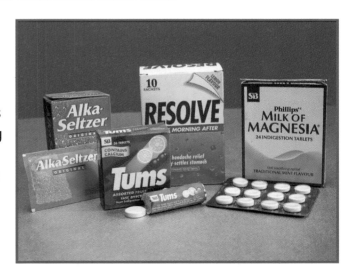

Problem soil

Some soils are slightly acidic. This is fine for plants such as heathers, which grow in places like the Yorkshire moors. The rhododendrons in the photo also like acidic soil. But most plants and food crops will not grow in acidic soil.

e Name a plant that prefers acidic soil.

f What would you do to neutralise an acidic soil?

Farmers and gardeners dig in a base called **lime** to neutralise the acidic soil. The photo on the right shows this.

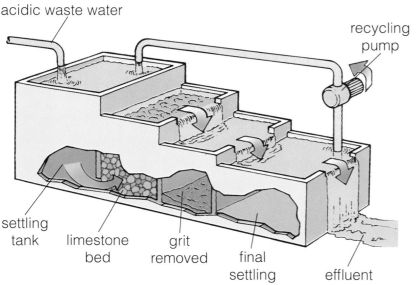

acidic waste water

recycling pump

settling tank   limestone bed   grit removed   final settling   effluent

Waste water treatment

Water from factories is often acidic or alkaline. One way of neutralising acidic waste water is to pass it over a bed of limestone, as shown on the left.

Questions

1. Copy and complete these sentences using the words below.

> **acid   alkali   base   neutralisation**

A _____ is the opposite of an _____. A _____ will react with an _____, taking away its acidity. The name of this chemical reaction is _____.

2. Val had acid indigestion. Roger told her not to drink cola. Why do you think he did this? What should she do?

Did you know?

Toothpaste neutralises the acid in your mouth which causes tooth decay.

3. Why doesn't stomach acid corrode the inside of your body?

4. What could you do to neutralise alkaline water from a factory?

For your notes

When you add a base to an acid, a chemical reaction called **neutralisation** takes place.

9

Salt on your chips, Sir?

Making a salt

Sodium hydroxide is an alkali. If you take solutions of hydrochloric acid and sodium hydroxide that have the same concentration, and mix equal volumes of them, the sodium hydroxide neutralises the acid. If you test the solution with universal indicator paper, you will find it has pH 7.

(a) What is the pH if you mix equal amounts of hydrochloric acid and sodium hydroxide?

If you leave the solution to evaporate, you will see crystals of salt. Yes, this is the salt you put on your chips! But, remember you must never taste anything in a laboratory.

Salt on your chips, Sir?

Neutralisation

When an acid is neutralised by a base, a salt and water are made. In science a **salt** is a substance we get from neutralisation. There are lots of different salts. In the reaction between hydrochloric acid and sodium hydroxide, sodium chloride (common salt) and water are made. You can write a word equation for this reaction:

> hydrochloric acid + sodium hydroxide $\longrightarrow$ sodium chloride + water

Hydrochloric acid and sodium hydroxide are the substances that reacted. We call them the reactants. We call the substances that are made in a chemical reaction the products. Sodium chloride and water are the products. The reactants are on the left of the word equation and the products are on the right.

It is important to use the correct amounts of acid and alkali in a neutralisation reaction. You can use an indicator or a pH meter to test for neutralisation.

(b) What is the pH after a neutralisation reaction between hydrochloric acid and sodium hydroxide?

Making other salts

There are lots of different types of salt. If you use other acids and alkalis, you get different salts. We can write a general word equation for the neutralisation reaction:

> acid + base $\longrightarrow$ salt + water
> **reactants**   **products**

Working out the name

To name a salt, start by taking the name of the metal from the base. For sodium hydroxide, take the name of the metal **sodium**. The second part comes from the acid – hydrochloric acid makes **chlorides**.

Chalk and acids

Chalk is **calcium carbonate**. Carbonates are bases, so they neutralise acids to make salts.

If you take a piece of chalk and drop it into hydrochloric acid, you will see bubbles. A salt is formed in the reaction. The bubbles are carbon dioxide gas:

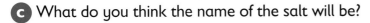

acid + carbonate ⟶ salt + water + carbon dioxide
   reactants   **products**

c What do you think the name of the salt will be?

Take the name of the metal from the base: and remember hydrochloric acid makes chlorides. The name of the salt is **calcium chloride**.

d Name the salt you would get if you reacted magnesium hydroxide with hydrochloric acid.

Questions

1. Copy and complete these sentences using the words below.

> bases   carbon dioxide   reacts   neutralisation

Acids react with _____ to form a salt and water. This reaction is called _____. Calcium carbonate _____ with acid, giving off _____ gas.

2. These cards show the reaction between an acid and a carbonate. They have become jumbled.

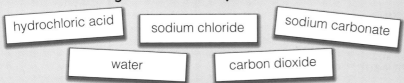

  a Use them to write a word equation.
  b Label the reactants and the products.
  c Name the salt that is produced.

3. Describe how you could remove the water from the salt after a neutralisation reaction.

For your notes

When an acid is neutralised by a base, a **salt** and water are formed.

The name of the salt comes from the names of the acid and the base used to make it.

Carbonates neutralise acids, forming a salt, water and carbon dioxide gas.

11

Corrosion

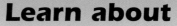
Hubble, bubble!

Some acids attack metals like iron and zinc. When a chemical eats away at a solid, we call it **corrosion**. Some metals are corroded faster than others.

A closer look at zinc

a What do you think will happen if you add zinc to acid?

Zinc reacts faster than some metals. If you add a few granules of zinc to some sulfuric acid in a beaker, it fizzes. The zinc is corroded and bubbles form. When all of the zinc has been used up, the bubbles stop.

b What do the bubbles tell you?

Acids react with some metals to make a salt and **hydrogen** gas. We can write a general word equation:

> acid + metal ⟶ salt + hydrogen
> **reactants** **products**

The word equation for the reaction between zinc and sulfuric acid is:

> sulfuric acid + zinc ⟶ zinc sulfate + hydrogen
> **reactants** **products**

c Which salt is made when zinc reacts with sulfuric acid?

Different metals

Jade and Itora did an experiment to investigate what happens when iron and copper are added to dilute sulfuric acid.

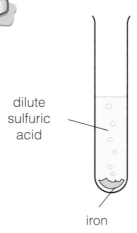

d Which metal did not react with sulfuric acid?

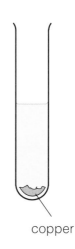

dilute sulfuric acid

iron   copper

Testing for hydrogen

We can collect some of the gas that bubbles off when zinc reacts with acid. We do this by passing the gas along a delivery tube and up through water. Hydrogen does not dissolve in water, and it floats.

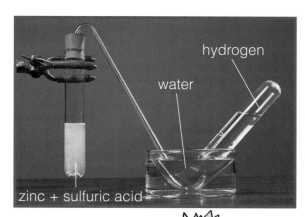

Once a test tube full of the gas has been collected, you can test it by putting a lighted splint near the top. Hydrogen gas is explosive, so you will hear a 'pop'! Hydrogen is the only gas that pops like this.

All acids contain hydrogen. The name of one acid gives us a clue about this.

e Which acid has part of the word hydrogen in its name?

Hydrochloric acid contains **hydro**gen and **chlor**ine and gets its name from both of these.

Acids and metal oxides

Copper does not react with dilute sulfuric acid, but black copper oxide does if you heat it. A blue solution of copper sulfate is formed. If you leave the solution to evaporate, you will see crystals of copper sulfate.

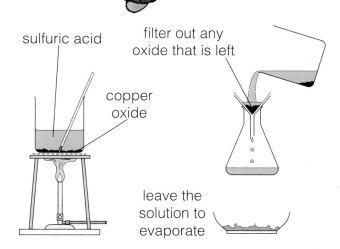

Acids react with metal oxides to make a salt and water. The general word equation is:

> acid + metal oxide → salt + water

The word equation for the reaction between sulfuric acid and copper oxide is:

> sulfuric acid + copper oxide → copper sulfate + water

Questions

1. Copy and complete the following word equations.
   a sulfuric acid + iron → _____ + hydrogen
   b sulfuric acid + _____ → magnesium sulfate + _____

2. What do you think would happen if you put an iron nail into a beaker of hydrochloric acid?

3. Describe the test for hydrogen.

For your notes

Some acids react with many metals, eating them away. This is called **corrosion**.

When an acid reacts with a metal, a salt and hydrogen gas are produced.

Hydrogen 'pops' with a lighted splint.

Acids react with many metal oxides, making a salt and water.

Acid in the air

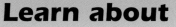

Rain again ...

Pure water is neutral, but if you test rainwater with universal indicator paper, you will find that it is slightly acidic.

ⓐ Rainwater does not burn your skin. Why not?

Rainwater is naturally acidic because some of the carbon dioxide in the air dissolves in the rain to make a weakly acidic solution of carbonic acid:

> carbon dioxide + water ⟶ carbonic acid

ⓑ Which gas in the air dissolves in rainwater to make an acidic solution?

Rock solid?

Over millions of years, slightly acidic rainwater has slowly dissolved away limestone rocks. Limestone is mainly made of calcium carbonate so it reacts with the acid. Holes and cracks begin to appear in the rocks, as shown in the photo. The general word equation for the reaction is:

> acid + carbonate ⟶ salt + water + carbon dioxide

Other rocks such as granite do not react with rainwater, but these rocks may also contain other substances which do react. This causes the rock to break up. Eventually the rock is completely broken up

into **soil**. When rocks break up by reacting with rainwater we call it **chemical weathering**.

ⓒ How is soil formed?

Adding to the acidity

Whenever fossil fuels are burned, such as gas, petrol, oil and coal, the rain is made more acidic.

Transplant problems

There is a big shortage of donor organs for transplant. The organs come from healthy people who have died in accidents such as car crashes. Not many families allow the organs of their dead relatives to be used for transplants.

Because of the shortage of organs for transplants, scientists are trying to use organs from other animals instead. Organs from baboons, chimpanzees, sheep and pigs have been transplanted into humans.

Pig organs are the best because they are most like our organs. They are the same size, and look very similar.

e Why are scientists trying to use organs from other animals instead of human organs?

f What animals have they used?

Questions

1. Copy and complete these sentences. Use words from the word wall to fill the gaps.

transplant	donate	organ
healthy		sick

An _____ is part of your body such as your heart or kidney. If one of your organs does not work properly, another person may _____ one of theirs.

When a _____ organ is taken out of one person and put inside the body of a _____ person, it is called a _____.

2. Both Julie's kidneys were damaged in an accident two years ago. Since then she has had to go to hospital three times a week. A dialysis machine in the hospital cleans her blood. It takes 5 hours each time. Without dialysis she would have died. Two weeks ago she had a kidney transplant. Write a newspaper article (like Leann's story) to describe what happened to Julie.

3. Design a poster to encourage people to carry organ donor cards.

Cells

All living things are made up of cells. There are two main types of cell, animal cells and plant cells. These cells have some very important differences.

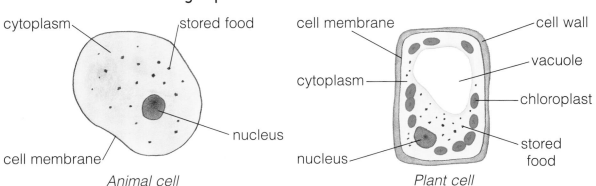

cytoplasm   stored food

nucleus

cell membrane

Animal cell

cell membrane   cell wall

cytoplasm   vacuole

chloroplast

nucleus   stored food

Plant cell

(a) What four things do all animal and plant cells have?

(b) What three things do only plant cells have?

Simple living things are made of only one cell. All the life processes happen in the single cell.

Many **algae** are single-celled organisms a bit like plants. You may have seen algae growing on tree trunks. They look like green dust.

Complicated organisms are made of millions of cells. In big organisms, different cells carry out different life processes. Different cells have different **functions**. This means that they do different jobs.

Inside your body there are over 200 different types of cell. The different types of cell look different. Each cell is adapted to have a special function. We say that the cells are **specialised**.

Types of cell

Epithelial cells make up the linings of your nose and throat. They are adapted to make mucus to trap dust and germs. Some of these cells also have tiny hairs called **cilia** which move the mucus out of your body.

not to scale

cilia

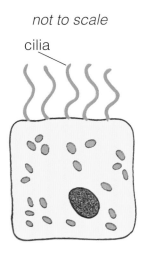

head

tail

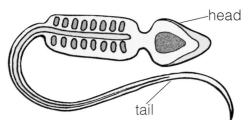

Sperm cells have long tails that wiggle. They are adapted to swim to the egg. The head has a pointed shape to help it burrow into the egg.

not to scale

protective
outer coating
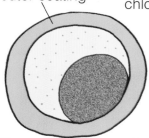

chloroplasts
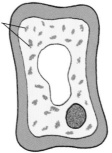

root hair
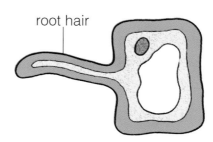

Egg cells are round and much bigger than a sperm cell. They have a protective layer so that only one sperm can get through.

Palisade cells in plant leaves have lots of chloroplasts to absorb as much light energy as possible for photosynthesis.

Root hair cells are in the roots of plants. They are adapted to have a large surface area to absorb as much water as possible.

Red blood cells are part of your blood. They have no nucleus and can be squashed so they can pass easily through small blood vessels. They are important for respiration.

c Why do sperm cells have tails?

d Make a table with three headings: 'Cell', 'Function', 'Adaptation'. Fill it in for each type of cell listed on these pages.

Tissues

In big organisms, there are groups of cells with the same function. We call this group of cells a **tissue**. An example is muscle tissue. This is made up of lots of muscle cells working together to move parts of your body. Each cell can only move a little, but thousands of cells working together can make your arm or leg move.

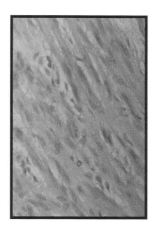

Onion skin is another example of a tissue. Lots of cells fit closely together to make a protective layer.

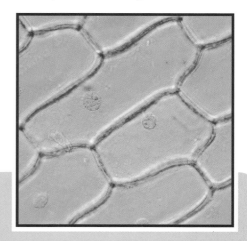

Questions

1. Explain where life processes happen in simple organisms.

2. Write out each cell and match it with the life process it is most involved with.

Cells	Life processes
sperm cell	nutrition
red blood cell	reproduction
palisade cell	respiration

3. Explain what a tissue is.

For your notes

Many cells are **specialised**.

Cells are adapted to their special **functions**.

A group of cells working together is called a **tissue**.

An organised system

Tissues working together

In plants and animals, different types of tissue are grouped together. The different types of tissue work together like cells do.

The function of your heart is to pump blood around the body. Your heart is made up of several different tissues. These tissues act together to make the heart work.

- The walls of the heart contain muscle tissue.
- Inside the heart are valves made of a different type of tissue. They only let the blood flow in one direction.
- The valves are held in place by another, stringy tissue.

A group of tissues working together is called an **organ**. Your heart is an example of an organ.

a What is an organ?

b What tissue are the walls of the heart made from?

Learn about

► Organs
► Organ systems

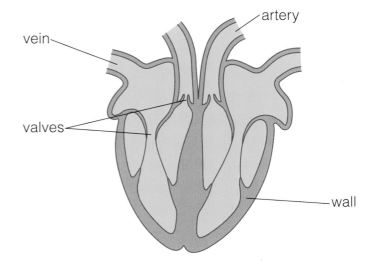

The circulatory system

The heart does not work alone. To do its job properly, it has to work with other cells, tissues and organs. A group of organs working together is called an **organ system**. The heart is part of an organ system called the **circulatory system**.

c What is meant by an organ system?

d Give an example of an organ system.

The circulatory system transports oxygen in the blood from the lungs to all the cells in the body. The heart pumps the blood containing red blood cells all around the body.

Blood goes around the body in tubes called **blood vessels**.

22

Lasting the distance

Using your muscles regularly when you exercise makes them stronger and able to work for longer. Compare the different runners in the photos.

The sprinter has large muscles that let her run very fast for a short time. The marathon runner cannot run as fast, but she can run for a long time without getting tired.

The athletes exercise in different ways. The sprinter will spend a lot of time in the gym lifting weights. This makes her muscles bigger and more powerful.

The marathon runner will spend a lot of time running, cycling and swimming. This type of exercise will increase the number of capillaries inside the muscles so she can run for longer.

Start of the 100 m sprint.   *The London Marathon.*

d Describe the differences between the muscles of a sprinter and of a marathon runner.

e Why do their muscles need to be different?

Different muscles for different functions

There are three different types of muscle in your body. Most of the muscle is the type you use to move. There is another type that moves food through your gut. A third type of muscle keeps your heart beating. It does not get tired like ordinary muscle.

Questions

1. What is the difference between a ligament and a tendon?

2. Copy and complete these sentences using the word **relaxes** or **contracts**.
   a To bend the arm, the biceps _____ and the triceps _____.
   b To straighten the arm, the biceps _____ and the triceps _____.

3. Roger wants to run the London Marathon. What kinds of exercise should he do to prepare for the race?

4. What is an antagonistic pair?

For your notes

Muscles are made of muscle tissue. They can **contract** and **relax**.

Bones move when a muscle contracts.

Muscles can only pull, they cannot push, so they work in **antagonistic pairs**.

Tharg, the alien?

It's the year 2516. The latest space probe has brought back an organism from a distant galaxy. The astronauts called the organism Tharg. A group of biologists are examining Tharg to find out what kind of organism he is, and whether his family might originally have come from Earth. They make measurements to collect data about him, so they can analyse it.

The body map

You have been asked to draw a scale diagram of Tharg's body on an A4 piece of paper. You have the measurements.

To do this you will have to use a **ratio** of **1:5**. A ratio is another way of giving a scale factor. For example, if you are measuring in centimetres, the ratio 1:5 means '1 cm on the scale diagram represents 5 cm in real life'. The ratio of the scale diagram to real life is 'one to five'. You have to say whether you are giving the ratio of the scale drawing to real life or the ratio of real life to the drawing. The ratio for your scale drawing means that Tharg is 5 times bigger than the drawing.

a Will you be scaling up or scaling down to draw a diagram of Tharg?

b What will you divide his real measurements by to get the measurements for your drawing? (This is your scale factor.)

c Copy the table and calculate the measurements for the scale diagram, using your scale factor from question **b**.

	Height	Arm length	Leg length	Foot length	Hand length
Tharg's size	92 cm	30 cm	35 cm	27 cm	5 cm
Scale drawing					

When you scale something up or down, all the parts of the scale drawing are scaled up or down by the same amount from real life.

d If you wanted to draw Tharg's index finger on your scale diagram, would you scale up or down?

e What scale factor would you use?

Simple ratios

You can see that a ratio has the number 1 on one side. If you know the length of Tharg's foot is 24 cm and you decide to draw it 6 cm long, you have a ratio of 'foot' to 'drawing' of 24:6. It is easier to do calculations if you always give ratios in the form 1:? or ?:1. To get the ratio into this form, you simplify it by dividing both numbers by the smallest number.

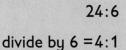

24:6

divide by 6 = 4:1

One of the biologists did a scan of Tharg to get an image of his heart. She also drew a large scale diagram of it, but has forgotten what ratio she used to draw it. She did not write the ratio on her diagram.

f If the width of the heart on the scan was 8 cm and the width in the drawing was 24 cm, what was the ratio she used?

g Did she scale up or down?

The blood count

Next the team wanted to find out how many green blood cells Tharg has in each 10 cm³ of blood. They took a small amount of blood, a **sample**, and found out how many blood cells were in that. We call this **sampling**.

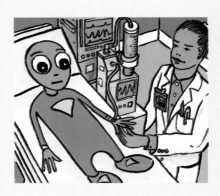

There are 25 green blood cells in every 1 cm³ of Tharg's blood. Now you can scale up to find out how many blood cells there are in 10 cm³ of blood.

The ratio of 'the volume you know about' to 'the volume you want to find out about' is: 1 cm³:10 cm³

h What do you need to scale up by?

i How many green blood cells are there in 10 cm³?

j How many green blood cells are there in 100 cm³? Explain how you got this answer.

Questions

1. Copy and complete the following sentences:

A ratio is a way of giving a _____ _____. If the ratio of a scale diagram to real life is 6:1, using centimetres this means _____ on the scale drawing represents _____ in _____ _____. You have to say whether you are giving the _____ of the scale drawing to real life or the _____ of real life to the scale drawing.

2. 1 cm³ of Tharg's blood also contains 9 pink blood cells. There are 1000 cm³ in 1 litre. How many pink blood cells are there in 1 litre? Explain how you work out your answer.

3. A pharmacist is going to give Tharg a drug which thins his blood. She knows the daily dose must not be more than 1 g per kg of Tharg's body. How do you think she might use ratios to work out what dose to give him?

One small step for man

Getting to know the Earth

For thousands of years people believed that the Earth was flat and it was surrounded by water. They thought that if a boat sailed too far away from land, it would fall off the edge of the world.

It was only about 30 years ago that a man could look down from space and see with his own eyes that the Earth is really a sphere.

The race into space

After the Second World War, the space race between the USA and the Soviet Union began. The first object to be sent into orbit around the Earth was called *Sputnik 1*, shown in the photo on the right. It was launched by the Soviet Union on 4 October 1957. *Sputnik 2* was launched later that year. It carried the first living thing to travel in space, a Russian dog called Laika.

(a) Why do you think a dog was used instead of a human in *Sputnik 2*?

On 12 April 1961, the Soviet Yuri Gagarin became the first person in space. He travelled in the spacecraft *Vostok 1*. He went round the Earth once in 1 hour 48 minutes before returning safely.

The first woman in space was also a Russian. Valentina Tereshkova was the pilot of *Vostok 6*. On 16 June 1963 she went around the Earth 48 times.

From the Earth to the Moon

In May 1961 the American president John F. Kennedy planned to get an American on the Moon before 1970. On 20 July 1969 *Apollo 11* made its successful journey to the Moon. Neil Armstrong and Edwin (Buzz) Aldrin went down to the Moon's surface. The landing was watched live by millions of people on television. Neil Armstrong's first words on the Moon were: 'That's one small step for man, one giant leap for mankind.'

(b) Why do you think it was a 'giant leap for mankind'?

What is out there?

In order to investigate our Solar System further, scientists have used space probes controlled by robots. In 1976, probes *Viking 1* and *Viking 2* sent back thousands of photographs of Mars so scientists could study its environment. More recently the Mars *Pathfinder* probe sent amazing pictures of the surface of Mars, such as the one here.

c Why do you think it has been necessary to use robots to study the Solar System further?

What's next?

Scientists are still exploring our Solar System. There are plans to build a spaceship that could take people to Mars. This would be very difficult, since it would take nearly a year to get there and another year to get back. The recent discovery of ice on the Moon means that it might be possible to maintain life on the Moon.

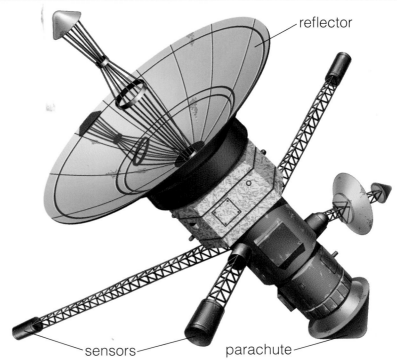

reflector

sensors   parachute

A space probe.

Questions

1. Why do you think the USA and Russia had a race to explore space?

2. **a** What problems would you have if you were a weightless astronaut in space?
   b What forces would act on you?

3. What could astronauts use the ice on the Moon for? Why might this be helpful?

4. Imagine you are the first person on the Moon. Write what you would say to the millions of people watching about being on the Moon and seeing the Earth from there.

Round the Sun

Orbiting the Sun

The Earth goes round the Sun once every year.
The path it takes is called an **orbit**. Our **Solar System** is made up of the Sun along with nine planets, including the Earth, orbiting the Sun. The Solar System also contains **asteroids**, **comets**, **meteors** and **meteorites** made of ice, rock, dust and gas. They are much smaller than planets.

a What does the name 'Solar System' describe? Why is it a good name?

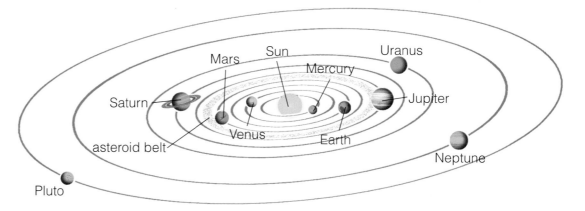

Planetary facts

Mercury is a small rocky planet that is closest to the Sun. It has no atmosphere and is very hot.

Venus is the hottest planet. It is rocky with an atmosphere of carbon dioxide.

Earth is a warm, rocky planet with water and an atmosphere of nitrogen and oxygen. It is the only planet we know about with living organisms.

Mars is a red, rocky, cold planet with an atmosphere of carbon dioxide.

Jupiter is a cold giant planet made mainly of liquids and gases. Jupiter is famous for its Great Red Spot. It has many moons.

Saturn is a cold giant planet made mainly from gases. It has beautiful rings around it and many moons.

Uranus is a cold pale green gas giant that has 15 moons and a number of rings like Saturn.

Neptune is a bluish gas giant with a cold atmosphere.

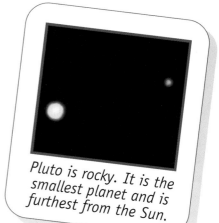

Pluto is rocky. It is the smallest planet and is furthest from the Sun.

b Suggest why it seems the Earth is the only planet suitable for life.

Differences between the planets

As you can see, there are many differences between the planets. As a result the conditions on each planet are very different. Their sizes also vary. Five of them are drawn to scale here.

Mercury 7 mm   Venus 18 mm   Earth 19 mm   Mars 10 mm   Pluto 3 mm

c Why do you think the four planets Jupiter, Saturn, Uranus and Neptune are not drawn on the page here?

How long is a year?

The Earth takes $365\frac{1}{4}$ days, or a **year**, to orbit the Sun. Mercury is the closest planet to the Sun and has the shortest year of only 88 Earth days. Pluto is the furthest away and takes 248 Earth years to orbit the Sun.

Questions

1. Make up a rhyme to help you remember the planets of the Solar System in order.

2. Choose the correct planet for each fact and write them down.

Planets
Earth   Jupiter   Mercury   Neptune
Venus   Saturn   Pluto   Uranus   Mars

Facts
Planet closest to the Sun
Planet furthest from the Sun
Hottest planet
Only planet we know that has life
Planet with a Great Red Spot

3. Explain why the planets nearer the Sun have a shorter year than the ones furthest away.

4. Look at what the nine planets are made from. Can you divide them into groups? Explain your answer.

For your notes

The **Solar System** is made up of the Sun and the nine planets along with their moons and other objects such as **comets**, **meteors** and **asteroids**.

The planets differ from each other in many ways such as diameter, distance from the Sun, what they are made of and the conditions there.

33

Shedding light on things

Seeing the light

Look at the photos. All these objects produce light.

Learn about

➤ Light
➤ Stars and planets
➤ Reflection

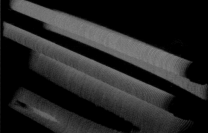

a Explain how we are able to see these things.

Light travels in a straight line, at a speed of 300 000 000 m/s. It is sometimes difficult to understand just how fast light is. If you have ever been to America you will know that it takes a long time to fly there. Even if you flew on Concorde, it would take 3 hours to fly to New York from London. Light is so fast that it gets there in less than a second.

The Sun as a star

Our Sun is a source of light for everyone on Earth. It is a star, and all stars are a source of light. It takes just 8.3 minutes for the light from the Sun to reach us. It is 150 million km away.

b Most of the space between the Sun and the Earth is empty space (a vacuum). Can light travel through a vacuum?

The photo opposite shows some stars in the night sky. When you look up at the stars, it's hard to believe that each one is a sun. Like all stars, our Sun is a huge ball of very hot gas. It is made mostly of hydrogen with some helium.

c Why is the Sun so important for life on Earth?

Seeing stars

Look back at the photo of the electric fire. It radiates heat energy which you can feel, and light energy which you can see. An orange fire is hotter than a red one. The Sun and stars are **luminous** which means they give out light. Some stars are red or orange, but the hotter ones are yellow or white. We can learn a lot about stars by looking at the light coming from them.

Colour	Appearance	Temperature
Red		3000 °C
Orange		4000 °C
Yellow		6000 °C
White		10 000 °C
Blue-white		20 000 °C

d Look at the table. The Sun is yellow at the surface. What is the temperature there?

Most of the stars we can see belong to our **galaxy**, the Milky Way. Our galaxy is a collection of 100 000 million stars.

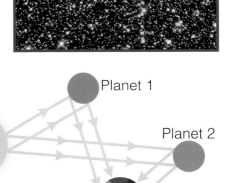

This picture of stars was taken by the Hubble telescope.

Seeing planets

Planets such as the Earth do not produce their own light. They are **non-luminous**. We only see planets because light from the Sun is reflected off them and reaches us. The diagram shows this.

e We can see the planet Venus, called the 'evening star', before it gets dark. We can only see stars at night. Why is this?

Planet 1

Planet 2

Sun

not to scale

Earth

Questions

1. Which of the following statements are true? Write out the ones that are true.
   a The temperature at the surface of the Sun is about 3000 °C.
   b Venus gives out the most light of all the planets.
   c Light can travel through a vacuum.
   d Light takes 8.3 seconds to reach us from the Sun.
   e We see the planets because the Sun's light is reflected off them.

2. Calculate how far light can travel in:
   a 1 minute   **b** 1 hour.

3. The next nearest star after our Sun is Alpha Centauri, 40 000 billion km away. Why do you think it takes longer for light from this star to reach us than light from the Sun?

4. The Pole Star is one of the brightest stars that we see in the sky from the UK. Suggest why it is so bright.

For your notes

The Sun and stars are sources of light.

We see planets and moons because they reflect light from the Sun to us.

Light travels in a straight line at 300 000 000 m/s.

Picturing the Solar System

Astronomy

People have always been fascinated by the Earth, the Moon, the Sun and the stars. Early sailors used to navigate by the stars. For instance, the Pole Star shows where the North Pole is. But they had very little idea how to explain what they saw. The study of planets, stars and other objects in space is called **astronomy**.

Pancake Earth?

Imagine you watch a ship sail away. You see it get smaller and then sink down from view. You think the Earth is flat and the ship has fallen off the edge. Later the ship and its sailors return.

a Explain how the Earth being a sphere fits with this evidence.

Earth at the centre?

In Ancient Greece, Aristotle thought the Earth was the centre of the universe and that everything including the Sun moved around the Earth. This model was called the **geocentric model** of the universe. 'Geo' comes from the Greek word for Earth. Ptolemy from Egypt drew a diagram of this model in the second century AD. For over 1000 years this theory was not challenged.

b Draw a simple diagram of the Earth and the Sun to represent the geocentric model of the universe.

Sun at the centre?

The Polish astronomer and churchman Copernicus (1473–1543) said that the Sun was at the centre of the Solar System. He said that the planets go around the Sun in circular orbits. This was called the **heliocentric model**. 'Helio' is from the Greek for Sun. The model is shown here.

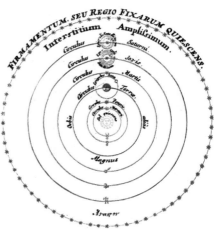

If astronomers had been able to look down on the universe and see the Sun, Earth and Moon, they would have seen exactly how they all moved. Instead, they had to make all the observations they could and use these as evidence for their models.

c Pretend you know nothing about the Solar System. Make a list of some of the evidence that astronomers in Copernicus' time might have observed from looking around them.

The Italian astronomer Galileo Galilei (1564–1642) made telescopes. These allowed him to see things in space magnified 30 times. He observed the movement of Jupiter's moons and this convinced him that the heliocentric theory of Copernicus was correct.

Refining the model

Tycho Brahe (1546–1601) was a Danish astronomer who did not invent or improve a model, but instead he made very accurate star charts. These included the positions of the planets, especially Mars. He collected the most accurate information about the planets so far.

The German mathematician Johannes Kepler (1571–1630) was an assistant to Tycho Brahe. Kepler used Brahe's observations to write his laws of planetary motion. Kepler's calculations showed that the planets move around the Sun in elliptical orbits, not circular ones as people had thought before. (An ellipse is a flattened circle.) But Kepler could not explain why this was so.

Tycho Brahe's observatory.

Sir Isaac Newton.

The British scientist Isaac Newton (1642–1727) explained why the planets had elliptical orbits when he published his law of gravitation in 1687.

Questions

1. What is the difference between the geocentric and heliocentric models of the universe?

2. Why was Galileo able to observe Jupiter's moons more accurately than anyone before him?

3. Tycho Brahe did not think of a new model of the universe. Why was his work important?

4. Produce a time line to show how ideas about the Solar System have changed. By each of these people, give a brief description of their contributions to the way ideas changed.

> **Ptolemy   Aristotle   Brahe**
> **Kepler   Copernicus**

For your notes

Many models or theories have been put forward over the centuries to explain the Solar System.

These models or theories have been changed and improved as new observations and evidence became available.

The **heliocentric model**, with the Sun at the centre of the Solar System, was first proposed by Copernicus in the fifteenth century.

Day and night

When the Sun shines on the Earth, only the side of the Earth facing the Sun gets any light. The other half of the Earth is in shadow.

The Earth spins on its **axis** once every 24 hours. The axis is an imaginary line that runs from the North Pole to the South Pole. As the Earth spins, the UK moves into the light.

ⓐ Look at the diagram. Is it daytime or night-time in the UK?

ⓑ What causes day and night?

You see the Sun appear to rise in the east. It appears to move across the sky and then set in the west.

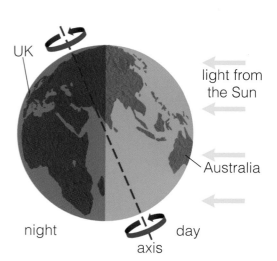

UK
light from the Sun
Australia
night
day
axis

ⓒ Explain why the Sun 'appears' to move. What is actually happening?

Through the night, the stars appear to move in a circle above our heads. To take this photo the camera shutter was left open for 4 hours.

Phases of the Moon

The Moon orbits the Earth once approximately every 28 days. Its shape appears to change. These changes are called the **phases of the Moon**.

day 7
day 4
day 11
Earth
day 14
day 1
light from the Sun
day 18
day 21
day 25

We see a full Moon when the Moon is on the opposite side of the Earth from

day 1   day 4   day 7   day 11   day 14   day 18   day 21   day 25

new Moon   first quarter   full Moon   last quarter

the Sun. We see a new Moon when the Moon is between the Sun and the Earth, so there is no sunlight shining on the side we see from Earth.

ⓓ Explain how we see the first and last quarters of the Moon.

Lunar eclipse

When the Earth is between the Sun and the Moon, we see a full Moon. Sometimes we also see a shadow of the Earth move across the Moon. This is called a **lunar eclipse**. Lunar eclipses can last for over an hour.

Lunar eclipses happen about twice a year. This is because the Moon's orbit is in a plane which is slightly tilted from the Earth's orbit. If they were both orbiting in the same plane, there would be a lunar eclipse every month.

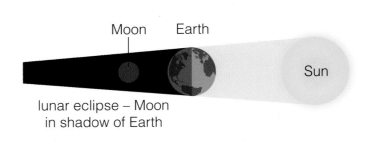

lunar eclipse – Moon
in shadow of Earth

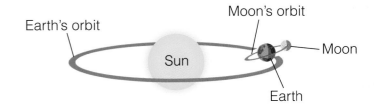

Solar eclipse

Sometimes the Earth and Moon are in a position in their orbits so that the Moon completely blocks the Sun's light from the Earth. This is a **solar eclipse**. The shadow of the Moon covers a small area of the Earth's surface in complete shadow. Here there is a **total eclipse**. Around the shadow is an area of partial shadow. Here there is a **partial eclipse**. You can only see a solar eclipse from a limited part of the Earth, and it never lasts more than 7 minutes.

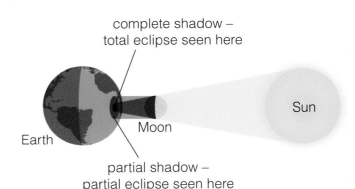

complete shadow –
total eclipse seen here

partial shadow –
partial eclipse seen here

Questions

1. Explain how day and night happen using the following words:

> 24 hours   axis   day   night
> east   west   sunrise   sunset

2. What would happen if the Earth turned more slowly on its axis?

3. Draw a diagram to show the positions of the Sun, Earth and Moon during:
 a a lunar eclipse **b** a solar eclipse.

4. Which lasts longer, a solar eclipse or a lunar eclipse?

For your notes

The Earth spins on its **axis** approximately once every 24 hours to give day and night.

The Moon orbits the Earth once every 28 days to give the **phases of the Moon**.

Sometimes the Earth is between the Sun and the Moon, and there is a **lunar eclipse**.

When the Moon blocks the Sun's light from reaching the Earth, there is a **solar eclipse**.

39

Earth and space

3.6

All in a year

Earth years

As well as spinning on its axis, the Earth orbits the Sun once every $365\frac{1}{4}$ days. This is called a **year**.

Every four years we have a **leap year**. A normal year has 365 days, while a leap year has 366 days. The extra day comes from adding together the extra four quarters of a day every four years.

The seasons

During the year, the climate in the UK changes. We have four **seasons**: spring, summer, autumn and winter.

a Describe how the climate in the UK changes with the seasons.

The axis the Earth spins on is slightly tilted, at $23\frac{1}{2}°$ from the vertical. The UK is on the top half of the Earth, called the **northern hemisphere**. When the northern hemisphere is tilted away from the Sun it is winter there, and when it is tilted towards the Sun it is summer.

b It is hotter in summer and cooler in winter. What else changes about the days with the seasons?

Learn about

➤ Seasons

Did you know?
The extra day is put in our calendar every four years on 29 February. If you were born on this day you only have a birthday every four years!

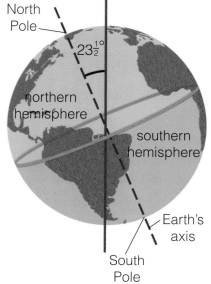

North Pole — $23\frac{1}{2}°$ — northern hemisphere — southern hemisphere — Earth's axis — South Pole

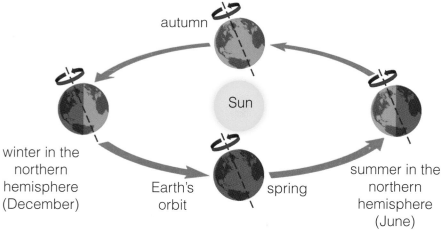

autumn — Sun — winter in the northern hemisphere (December) — Earth's orbit — spring — summer in the northern hemisphere (June)

Life at the Poles

When it is summer in the northern hemisphere, the Sun never completely sets at the North Pole. But in the winter there is a period when it never rises.

c Explain what happens at the South Pole when it is:
i summer at the North Pole
ii winter at the North Pole.

Daylight hours

In midsummer we have long days and short nights. 21 June is called the **summer solstice**. This is the longest day, and the Sun is highest in the sky. In midwinter we have short days and long nights. 21 December is the **winter solstice**. This is the shortest day, and the Sun is lowest in the sky.

Sun high in the sky at midday in midsummer – long days, short nights

Sun lower in the sky at midday in midwinter – short days, long nights

d i What is the shortest day called?

ii Is the northern hemisphere tilted towards the Sun or away from the Sun on the shortest day?

Seasonal stars

Look at the diagram on the opposite page which explains the seasons. Imagine that it is dark as you look out at the stars in June and December. In June, the UK is facing into space in one direction and in December it is facing into space in the opposite direction. This means we see different stars in each direction. There are some stars we see all year round, but there are others we only see in the summer or winter.

In December we see Orion.

In June we see Cygnus.

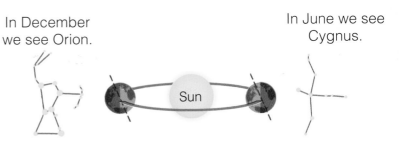

Sun

e Why can we see different stars in summer and winter?

Questions

1. Copy and complete the sentences below.

   The Earth's axis is slightly tilted at _____. This tilt of the Earth causes the _____. In the UK it is summer when the northern hemisphere is tilted towards the _____. On 21 June the _____ _____ happens. On this date we have the longest _____ and shortest _____. The shortest day occurs on _____ _____.

2. Draw diagrams to show the shadow from a tree in the UK at midday on:
   a 21 June **b** 21 December.

3. Australia is in the southern hemisphere. What season is it in Australia when it is summer in the UK?

4. Make a list of all the changes between winter and summer that we notice in the UK.

For your notes

It takes the Earth $365\frac{1}{4}$ days or a **year** to orbit the Sun.

The Earth is slightly tilted at $23\frac{1}{2}°$ from the vertical. This causes the **seasons** or changes in the climate.

The stars we see in the night sky change with the seasons because we are facing a different way into space.

In orbit

Natural satellites

A **satellite** is an object that orbits a larger object. The Earth and the other planets of the Solar System are natural satellites of the Sun. The Moon is a natural satellite of the Earth. The Moon goes around the Earth just like a ball on a string would go around you if you swung it around your head.

Gravitational force

The planets are kept in orbit by the **gravitational force** between them and the Sun. Because the Sun is so massive, it has a huge gravitational pull which keeps all the planets orbiting round it. Objects with a big mass give a big gravitational pull. Objects that are close together have a stronger pull on each other than objects further away.

a The Earth has a larger mass than the Moon. Which gives the bigger gravitational pull on objects near it?

b Explain why the Moon orbits in the gravitational pull of the Earth rather than that of the Sun.

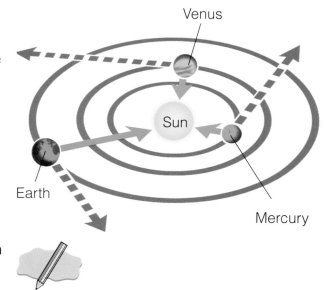

Venus

Sun

Earth

Mercury

Artificial satellites

There are also **artificial satellites** around the Earth. These have been launched by us. They go around the Earth in a similar way to the Moon.

A satellite is launched by a rocket or the Space Shuttle. It needs a big force to get into orbit. The higher the orbit of the satellite, the more force is needed to get it there.

c What would happen to a satellite if it was launched with too small a force?

Geostationary and polar orbits

Artificial satellites are put into different orbits depending on the job they are going to do. Some orbit the Earth at the same speed as the Earth is turning on its axis. These are called **geostationary satellites**. Geostationary satellites orbit the Earth once every 24 hours, which means they stay in the same place over the Earth's surface. Other satellites are in orbits that take them over the North and South Poles. These are called **polar orbits**.

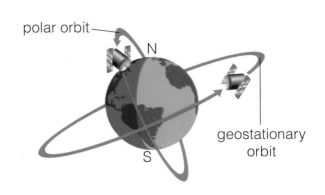

d With a partner, discuss how you could make a simple model out of balls of paper to show how a geostationary satellite stays over the same place on the Earth's surface.

Uses of artificial satellites

Artificial satellites are useful to us in many ways:

1. **Communication satellites** send radio, TV and telephone messages around the world. These are geostationary satellites.

2. **Exploration satellites** carry telescopes and can take clear pictures of planets. They can also look at the universe. The Hubble telescope is a good example.

3. **Weather satellites** take pictures of cloud formations and send them to Earth. This helps the weather forecasters to predict our weather.

4. **Navigation satellites** are used by ships, cars and planes to find their position on the Earth. They can give the position to within 10 metres.

Questions

1. **a** What is a gravitational force?
   b What does the strength of the gravitational force between two objects depend on?

2. What is the advantage of a satellite that is in:
   a a geostationary orbit?
   b a polar orbit?

3. Prepare a presentation for the rest of your class about the importance of satellites to us.

For your notes

A **satellite** is an object that orbits a larger object.

The planets are held in orbit around the Sun by the **gravitational force** of the Sun.

There are natural satellites such as the Earth and planets orbiting the Sun, and the Moon orbiting the Earth.

Artificial satellites are machines launched into space by people. They are used for communicating across our planet or studying space.

The Solar System

Class 8J were studying the Solar System. They made models to show the Solar System. They used the information in the table. The Sun is 1392000 km in diameter.

Planet	Diameter (to nearest 1000 km)	Average distance from Sun (to nearest 1000000 km)
Mercury	5000	58000000
Venus	12000	108000000
Earth	13000	150000000
Mars	7000	228000000
Jupiter	143000	780000000
Saturn	121000	1427000000
Uranus	51000	2871000000
Neptune	50000	4504000000
Pluto	2000	5900000000

Relative sizes

Ian, Karl and Darren made a model showing the sizes of the planets. Darren brought in a yellow beach ball to be the Sun. Karl and Ian brought in other balls to be the planets.

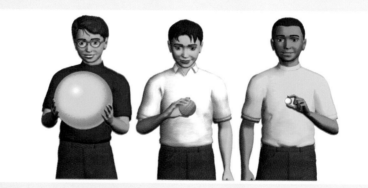

Ball	Diameter in cm
Beach	40
Basketball	23.9
Football	22.3
Netball	21.3
Volleyball	20.7
Cricket	7.3
Tennis	6.4
Squash	4.4
Golf	4.3
Table tennis	3.8

(a) Karl also brought in a rugby ball, but they did not use it. Why not?

They put the balls in order with the biggest first and the smallest last, as shown in the table. The beach ball stands for the Sun.

(b) Decide which ball should stand for each planet.

Ian, Karl and Darren showed their model to the rest of the class. The model shows the sizes of the Sun and the planets. The class **evaluated** the model. First, they said the good things about the model.

c Suggest two other good points about the model.

The class then thought of ways to improve the model.

d Suggest two ways to improve the model.

Ian, Karl and Darren decided to make a scale model. They made a ball of clay 2 mm in diameter for Pluto. Using the same scale, Jupiter will be 143 mm and the Earth will be 13 mm.

e What will be the diameter of: **i** Saturn? **ii** Mars? **iii** the Sun?

The balls are spheres, like the sun and the planets.

Uranus and Neptune are almost the same size, and the netball and the volleyball are almost the same size.

Relative distances

Serena, Joyce and Parveen made a model showing the distances of the planets from the Sun. They put labels on string to show the positions of the planets. They used 1 mm of string for every 1 000 000 km. Pluto is 5 900 000 000 km from the Sun, so Pluto was 5900 mm, or 5.9 m, along the string.

f Where did they put the labels for: **i** Mercury? **ii** Earth? **iii** Jupiter?

The class then evaluated the model.

g Read the comments on the right. Divide them into 'good points' and 'problems with the model'.

Sizes and distances

Class 8J wanted to build one model to show both the sizes of the planets and their distances from the Sun.

h Using the scale 1 mm = 1000 km, how far will Pluto be from the Sun in the class model?

i Is it possible to build a model that shows both the sizes of the planets and their distances from the Sun? Give reasons for your answer.

- *It shows how close together the inner planets are, and the big gaps between the outer planets.*
- *The distances are to scale.*
- *Sometimes the distances are shorter and sometimes they are longer. Sometimes Pluto is inside Neptune's orbit.*
- *It shows the planets in a straight line.*
- *It makes the planets look too close together. They are often on opposite sides of the sun.*

Questions

1. Study the information opposite about the Earth and the Moon.

Draw a scale diagram, or make a model, of the Earth and Moon with a scale of 1 mm = 1000 km.

The average (mean) distance from the Earth to the Moon is 384 000 km.

The diameter of the Earth is 13 000 km.

The diameter of the Moon is 3500 km.

45

It's all Greek to me!

All materials are made up from tiny particles.

The first scientist to have this idea was called Leucippus. He lived in Ancient Greece around 400 BC. He had a student called Democritus who carried on his work. It was very difficult to prove their ideas. The particles were much too small to see. Not many people believed them.

a Imagine that you lived in Ancient Greece. Would you have believed them? Explain your reasons.

Everything is made up of particles.

Snooker balls

The idea of particles was then forgotten for over 2000 years. In 1808 a British scientist called John Dalton had some new ideas. He thought that particles were round and hard, like small snooker balls. He said that these tiny particles could not be split up and made any smaller. He called them atoms.

Substances that are elements contain only one type of atom. Substances that are compounds contain more than one type of atom joined together.

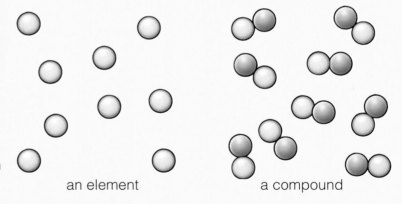

an element   a compound

b What name did Dalton give to the particles in matter?

c What is the difference between an element and a compound?

A new model

Other scientists began to use Dalton's idea of particles to explain why solids, liquids and gases behaved in the way they did. They produced a model of how particles were arranged in each state of matter. This model was called the **particle theory**.

Solids are hard substances that keep their shape. They cannot be squashed. The scientists' model said that the particles in a solid are very close together and joined quite strongly. The particles cannot move much. They can only jiggle about.

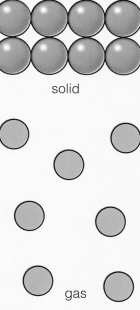
solid

Liquids are runny substances. They change their shape to fit their container. The model said that the particles in a liquid are not joined together as strongly as they are in a solid. This means that they can slip and slide past each other. This allows the liquid to change shape. You cannot squash a liquid, so the particles must still be very close together.

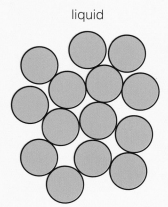
liquid

Gases are not very dense and can be squashed quite easily. The model said that the particles in a gas must be very far apart. Gases fill up all of the space they are in, so the particles must be able to move around very quickly and easily.

gas

d Why is it difficult to squash a solid? Use the word 'particle' in your answer.

e Describe the differences between the way the particles are arranged in a solid and in a gas.

Small is beautiful

For many years, scientists could not see atoms because they were far too small. Recently, new and very powerful microscopes have allowed us to see atoms for the first time. Atoms are the smallest things that we have been able to see under a microscope. The photo shows carbon monoxide seen through this new microscope. The particles have been arranged using a special machine to make a picture of a stick person.

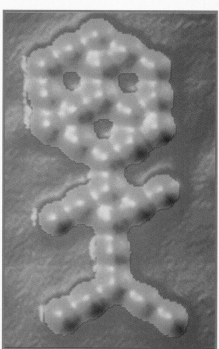

Questions

1. **a** Find a word on these two pages that means a particle that cannot be split up and made any smaller.
   b Find a word that means a substance made of only one type of particle.
   c Find a word that means a substance made of more than one type of particle joined together.

2. Draw a time line to show how ideas about the atom have changed.

3. Give a presentation for the rest of your class about the particle theory.

Making new materials

Elements

Everywhere you look there are substances we call **chemicals**. All chemicals are made up of atoms. Elements are chemicals that are made from only one type of atom. Pure copper contains only copper atoms and pure sulfur contains only sulfur atoms. In total, 118 elements have been discovered so far.

But as you know, there are many thousands of different substances that we use every day. Some examples are oil, plastic, metals, dyes, medicines and food, to name just a few. All these materials are chemicals and they are all made from the 118 elements.

Compounds

A compound is a substance made up of more than one type of atom. The different atoms are joined together chemically.

There are thousands of compounds. One simple one is hydrogen sulfide, made from hydrogen and sulfur atoms.

(a) What is a compound? Give an example.

hydrogen + sulfur → hydrogen sulfide
element   element   compound

Molecules

In hydrogen sulfide, the different atoms are joined up to make particles called **molecules**. Each hydrogen sulfide molecule contains two hydrogen atoms and one sulfur atom.

Some elements are made up of molecules. These molecules are made from only one type of atom. Hydrogen gas is made up of hydrogen molecules. These contain pairs of hydrogen atoms, joined together chemically.

Substances made up of molecules are often gases or liquids. Oxygen and nitrogen are gases that are made up of molecules. Chlorine is another element that has molecules containing two atoms joined together.

Water is a compound made up of molecules. Water is made up of the elements hydrogen and oxygen. We can write a word equation to show how water is formed:

hydrogen + oxygen → water
element element compound
                    (hydrogen oxide)

We can also draw a circle to represent each atom in the molecules, as shown on the right.

hydrogen   oxygen   water

Carbon dioxide is another compound made up of molecules.

b Name: **i** an element made up of molecules
ii a compound made up of molecules.

c What is the ratio of the different atoms in a carbon dioxide molecule?

carbon dioxide

Chemistry's code

Instead of drawing a circle for each atom, we can show a reaction using just the symbol for the element. Glucose is an example of a more complex molecule. Imagine drawing all these circles!

The 6 shows there are 6 carbon atoms.

The 6 shows there are 6 oxygen atoms.

$$C_6H_{12}O_6$$

The 12 shows there are 12 hydrogen atoms.

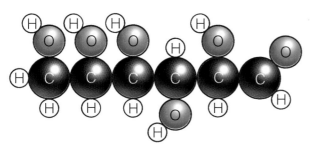

You can see that it is much easier to write letters to represent a glucose molecule.

CCCCCCHHHHHHHHHHHHOOOOOO

But keeping track of how many letters you have written isn't easy either. Instead, we write numbers against the symbols to show how many atoms there are of each element.

d What is the ratio of the different atoms in a glucose molecule?

We show a molecule of water as H_2O or a molecule of carbon dioxide as CO_2. This is the **formula** of the compound.

e Use this formula method to write equations for producing:
i water from hydrogen and oxygen
ii carbon dioxide from carbon and oxygen.

Questions

1. Chlorine reacts with hydrogen to form hydrogen chloride gas, which has the formula HCl.
a Write a word equation for this reaction showing the molecules.
b Beneath the word equation, write the formula equation for this reaction.

2. Methane has the formula CH_4.
a Draw a methane molecule using circles.
b What is the ratio of the different atoms in the molecule?

For your notes

There are about 100 elements that are combined in different ways to make all the materials we have.

Different types of atom are joined together to make **compounds**.

A **molecule** is a group of atoms joined together.

Elements, compounds and molecules can be represented by **formulae**.

Matter

4.3

All change!

Melting and freezing

The diagram shows a temperature probe in a test tube of ice. The computer will draw a graph of the temperature of the ice as it gets warmer. The graph that you might see is shown on the right.

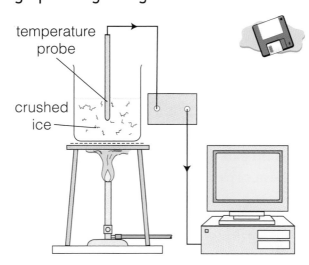

temperature probe

crushed ice

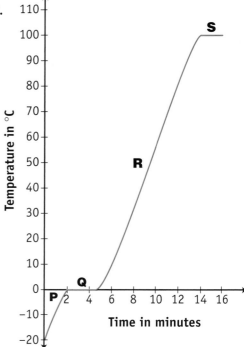

At the beginning, the ice is a solid. The molecules are close together and vibrating slightly. They are held together by pulling forces between the molecules. Energy from the flame gives the molecules in the ice more energy, so they vibrate faster. As they vibrate faster, the temperature of the ice rises, as shown on the graph.

(a) What happens to the molecules as the ice gets warmer?

When the temperature of the ice reaches 0 °C, something special happens. Energy from the flame makes the molecules vibrate so much that some of the pulling forces holding them together are broken. Some of the molecules begin to move around each other freely. The solid starts to turn into a liquid.

The temperature of the mixture of ice and water stays at the **melting point** until all the ice turns into water. The energy from the flame is still being used to break some of the pulling forces.

Learn about

- Changes of state
- Energy
- Temperature

Then the temperature starts to rise again as energy makes the molecules move even faster.

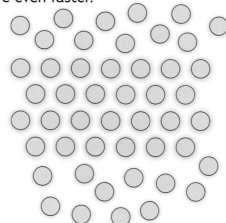

(b) Explain what happens to the molecules in ice at 0 °C.

It is possible to carry out the reverse of this experiment and see what happens as water is cooled down to melting point.

(c) What happens to the molecules as you cool down liquid water?

Different directions

Water melts at 0°C. It also freezes at 0°C. This is a reversible process. If you are giving the molecules energy, the substance is melting. If you take energy away, the substance is freezing.

giving the molecules energy = melting
taking energy away from the molecules = freezing

Boiling

In liquid water, there are still some pulling forces holding the molecules together. As you heat water, the energy makes the molecules roll around each other faster and faster. At 100°C another change happens. The molecules are moving so fast that the pulling forces between them are broken and they are free to fly about. The liquid becomes a gas called steam. The temperature stays at 100°C, the **boiling point**, until all the liquid becomes gas.

Condensing

Condensing is the opposite of boiling. Gas cools down and becomes a liquid.

d Draw some diagrams to show what happens to the molecules as steam condenses to water.

Evaporation

In a liquid, the molecules are all moving around at different speeds. Some of the molecules at the surface get enough energy to break the pulling forces and move away from the surface of the liquid. Some of the liquid has evaporated – it has turned into a gas.

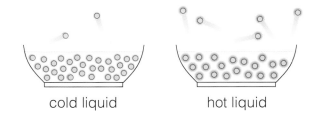

cold liquid   hot liquid

For your notes

Ice melts when the molecules are given enough energy to break the pulling forces which hold them together.

Water freezes when the molecules lose energy and become joined by pulling forces.

Water boils when the molecules have enough energy to overcome the pulling forces between them.

Condensing is the opposite of boiling. Gas molecules lose energy and gas becomes liquid.

Evaporation only happens at the surface of a liquid.

Questions

1. Copy the table and put these changes of state into the correct column:

   melting condensing freezing evaporating boiling

Molecules take in energy	Molecules lose energy

2. Design an experiment to find the melting point of sulfur. What safety precautions would you need to take?

3. Write a description of what happens to the molecules and pulling forces when water freezes.

Wandering particles

What's that smell?

This perfume has a lovely scent.

This onion is making my eyes water!

This air freshener makes the whole room smell nice.

All of the things in the photos give off smells. Quite often you can smell something even when you are not near it. You would be able to smell the air freshener all over the room. It gives off a gas. Gases are made of particles which move and spread out to fill all of the space available.

You cannot see what is making the smell in the air. The smell is caused by tiny particles that are too small to see. But special cells in your nose can detect these particles.

Diffusion

If someone let off a stink bomb in a corner, people near it would be the first to smell it. Gradually people further and further away would smell it. Eventually everybody would notice the smell.

The stink bomb contains a bad-smelling liquid. When you let the stink bomb off, this liquid evaporates and becomes a gas. The smelly gas particles mix with particles in the air. The smelly particles keep moving in all directions. Eventually they spread through the room.

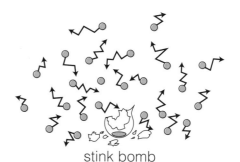

stink bomb

This movement is called **diffusion**. It happens by itself, you don't need to mix or stir the substances.

ⓐ What is diffusion?

ⓑ Why would a person sitting near the stink bomb smell it before someone far away?

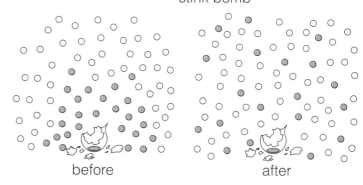

before   after

Diffusion in liquids

Diffusion doesn't only happen in gases. The photos above show diffusion happening in a liquid. Particles in a liquid are able to move about a little, but not as much as in a gas. You can see the purple colour spread out as the particles gradually move and mix into the water. Eventually all of the water is purple.

c Why is diffusion faster in a gas than in a liquid?

d Why was the purple colour at the top of the beaker stronger at the end than it was at the beginning?

Hot and cold

Particles move faster when they are hot than when they are cold. This means that diffusion will happen faster in a hot liquid. The particles will mix more quickly.

e Would a stink bomb spread quicker on a cold day or a hot day? Explain why.

Questions

1. Copy and complete these sentences. Use words from the word wall to fill the gaps.

spread	directions	diffusion
particles	smells	mixing

Gas _____ can move and _____ out in all _____. Eventually they spread out evenly in the air. This mixing is called _____.

2. Use your knowledge of diffusion to explain why you might smell an air freshener from the other side of the room.

3. Helen noticed that her green bubble bath spread quicker in a hot bath that it did in a cold bath. Explain to her why this happens.

4. Why does diffusion not happen in a solid?

For your notes

Substances spread out in a gas or a liquid as their particles move and mix. This is called **diffusion**.

Diffusion happens faster in a hotter liquid or gas. This is because the particles are moving faster.

Size matters

Mercury rising

The photo shows a thermometer. Some thermometers contain a metal called mercury. Mercury is different from most metals because it is a liquid at room temperature.

When it is hot, the mercury appears to move up the thermometer.

When it is cold, the mercury appears to move down the thermometer.

The column of mercury gets bigger and smaller. The particle theory can be used to explain why this happens.

Expanding

As the mercury is heated up, its particles are given heat energy. This energy is changed into movement energy. This means that the particles move around more and take up more space. We say the mercury has **expanded**.

Because each particle takes up more space, the column of mercury gets longer. The glass tube stops it from expanding in other directions. We see the top edge of the mercury column move up the thermometer.

a Why does the mercury appear to move up the thermometer when it gets hotter?

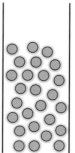

At lower temperatures, the particles only vibrate a little.

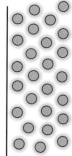

At higher temperatures, the particles are the same size but they vibrate more and take up more space. The mercury expands.

Contracting

If you cool the mercury down, the opposite happens. The particles lose movement energy. They vibrate less and take up less space.

Because each particle takes up less space, the mercury column gets shorter. We say that the mercury has **contracted**. We see the top edge of the mercury column move down the thermometer.

b Why does the mercury appear to move down the thermometer when it gets cooler?

Expanding bridges

Engineers need to know about expansion and contraction in solids when they build things. Changes in temperature can affect the way building materials behave.

In some railway lines, there is a gap between the pieces of track to give the metal room to expand on hot days. If the gaps were not there, the track would buckle and bend.

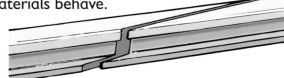

Power cables are never tight between pylons. The cable is always slightly loose. This means that on very cold days, when the cable contracts, it does not pull the pylons together.

The ends of many bridges are not fixed to the rest of the road. There are gaps at the ends to allow the bridge to expand. Sometimes the ends are placed on rollers to help them move as they expand, as shown below.

c Why do some railway tracks have gaps in them?

d What would happen if the bridge was fixed at both ends?

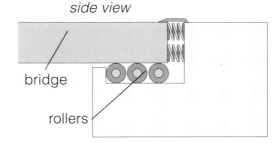

side view

bridge

rollers

Questions

1. Copy and complete these sentences. Use words from the word wall to fill the gaps.

slower	contracted	smaller	faster	apart
liquid	bigger	expanded	particle	space

If you heat up a substance, its particles move _____. The particles take up more _____. The substance gets _____. It has _____.

If you cool a substance down, its particles move _____. The particles take up less _____. The substance gets _____. It has _____.

2. Why does a metal ruler give a different measurement on a cold day than on a hot day?

3. Jess could not get the lid off her jam jar. She put the lid under the hot tap for a minute and then tried again. It came off easily. Explain why this happened.

For your notes

When you heat a substance, the particles vibrate more and take up more space. The substance **expands**.

When you cool a substance, the particles vibrate less and take up less space. The substance **contracts**.

Under pressure

Pump it up

Inside this balloon are millions of air particles.
These gas particles are moving around in all directions.

Every time they hit the side of the balloon, they give the rubber a tiny push. Each push is quite small, but lots of particles all pushing at the same time adds up to quite a lot of force.

The force against the side of the balloon causes **gas pressure**. The balloon is kept in shape by the pressure of the gas inside it.

a How do the particles move in a gas?

b What causes gas pressure?

Learn about

➤ Gas pressure

Air pressure

Air is a gas. The particles are all around us and we are always being hit by them. They cause **air pressure** (or atmospheric pressure). We don't usually feel the air pressure because the pressure within our bodies balances the pressure outside.

Wind is caused by air rushing in from an area of high pressure to an area of low pressure. We see this when air rushes out of a hole in a balloon.

c Explain why air rushes out of hole in a balloon by comparing the pressure inside the balloon and the air pressure outside.

Did you know?
Bicycle tyres filled with air were invented by John Dunlop in 1888.

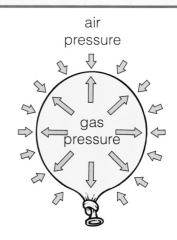

Heat it up

If you heat a gas inside a syringe, the particles have more energy and so they move around faster and move further apart. They hit the sides of the syringe more often. They also hit them harder. The pressure of the gas inside the syringe increases if the plunger can't move.

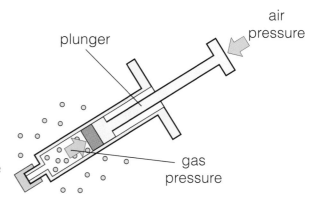

But the air pressure outside stays the same. The force on the inside of the plunger is bigger than the force on the outside of it. The plunger will move out, if you allow it to, until the pressure inside is the same as the air pressure outside. The forces on the plunger are now balanced. The gas has expanded.

d Why does the plunger move out when the gas is heated?

e What do you think would happen to the plunger if the gas in the syringe got colder?

When you heat a gas in a syringe, it becomes less dense. This is because there are still the same number of particles, but they have moved further apart, so they take up a bigger volume.

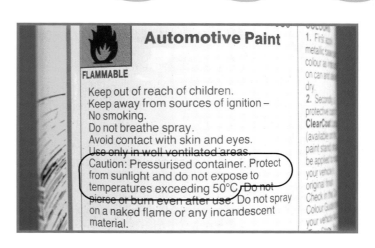

Too much pressure

If you heat a gas inside a container that cannot get bigger, then the gas pressure will increase. If the pressure gets too high, then the container may explode.

Questions

1. Copy and complete these sentences. Use words from the word wall to fill the gaps.

softer	harder	often	particles	hitting
push	pull	decrease	increase	less

Gas pressure is cause by the _____ of a gas _____ the sides of the container.

When particles hit the sides of the container they give the container a little _____.

If you warm up a gas, the particles will hit the container _____ and more _____. The gas pressure will _____.

2. Why does a balloon get bigger when it is warmed up?

3. Dot noticed that the tyres on her bike were harder on a hot day than they were on a cold day. Why do you think this happens?

For your notes

Gas pressure is caused by the gas particles hitting the sides of the container.

When you heat a gas, the particles hit the sides of the container more and the pressure goes up. When you cool the gas, the pressure goes down.

If you heat a gas in a container that can get bigger, the gas expands. It becomes less dense.

Air pressure is caused by air particles all around us and we are always being hit by them.

How much will dissolve?

The photo shows copper sulfate dissolving in water. Look at the diagram. The copper sulfate solution contains particles from the copper sulfate (blue), each surrounded by water molecules (white).

Saturation and solubility

You can add more and more copper sulfate crystals until no more will dissolve. The solution is then saturated. You can see some copper sulfate crystals in the bottom of the beaker.

(a) How do you know that a solution is saturated?

Scientists measure what mass of a substance will dissolve in 100 cm³ of solvent at a certain temperature. This is called the **solubility** of the substance. Each substance has a different solubility. For example, 38 g of salt will dissolve in 100 cm³ of water at 25 °C. In most cases, the solubility of a solid increases when the temperature rises.

Learn about

► Dissolving
► Solubility

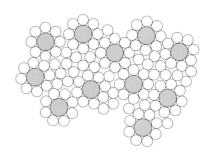

Mass of salt.

Mass of water.

Mass of salt solution.

Where does it go?

Look at the photos. Matter is not lost when you make a solution. You have the same mass of solute and solvent as you started with. We say that the mass has been **conserved**.

Different temperatures

The solubility of a substance depends on the temperature of the solvent. Look at the graph. It shows how much of substances **X** and **Y** will dissolve in 100 cm³ of water at different temperatures.

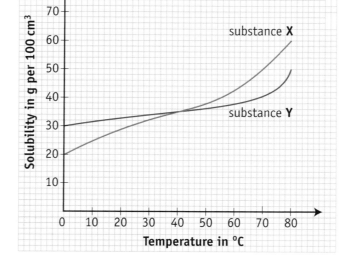

b How much of substance **X** dissolves at 70 °C?

c How much of substance **Y** dissolves at 10 °C?

d Which substance is the more soluble at 60 °C?

Temperature also affects how quickly a substance will dissolve. At higher temperatures, the solvent molecules have more energy and move more quickly. The solvent molecules hit the lumps of solid more often and harder, knocking off the outer particles more easily.

Cooling off

If you cool a saturated solution of copper sulfate, crystals of the copper sulfate are formed again. Some of the solute comes out of solution. There is still the same total amount of copper sulfate there.

Look at the graph on the opposite page. At 80 °C, 60g of **X** dissolves. At 55 °C, 40g of **X** dissolves.

e How much **X** would crystallise out if you cooled a saturated solution from 80 °C to 55 °C?

Different solvents

Different solutes dissolve in different solvents. For example, salt dissolves in water but not in paraffin. It is insoluble in paraffin.

Each substance has a different solubility. This allows scientists to separate mixtures by chromatography. The more soluble solutes move with the solvent as it creeps up the paper. The less soluble solutes hardly move from the spot where they were put on the paper.

Chromatography can also use different solvents. The chromatograms below show ink from two different pens. The experiment was carried out with two different solvents, water and ethanol.

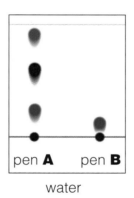 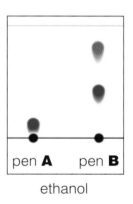

water   ethanol

Questions

1. Copy and complete these sentences. Use words from the word wall opposite to fill the gaps.

   | saturated | spaces | particles |
   | dissolve | crystals | solubility |

   When no more of a substance will _____, the solution is _____. You can tell that no more will dissolve because you can see _____ on the bottom of the beaker. The amount of a substance that will dissolve is called the _____.

2. If you add 10g of salt to 100g of water, what is the mass of the final solution? Explain your answer.

3. How might you use a solvent to separate a mixture of salt and sand?

4. Look at the chromatograms above. Which pen is the best to use for labelling your PE kit? Explain your answer.

For your notes

Solubility is the amount of a substance that will dissolve.

The solubility of a substance changes with temperature.

Mass is always **conserved** in solutions.

Some substances are insoluble in certain solvents.

Scientific models

Models

The word 'model' can mean lots of different things to us. You might think of a fashion model on a catwalk, or a model aeroplane. When scientists talk about a model, they usually mean a way of showing how something works or looks that they cannot see or touch.

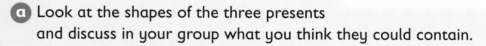
Christmas presents

On Christmas Eve, Jackie's six-year-old brother Matt had gone to bed. Jackie was looking at the presents for him under the Christmas tree. She couldn't open them, but she wanted to try and find out what was in them.

First she just looked at three presents for Matt and thought about their shapes. She tried to decide what they might contain.

a Look at the shapes of the three presents and discuss in your group what you think they could contain.

Next she picked up the three presents and felt how heavy they were. After that she squeezed them.

b What else could she do with the presents, apart from open them, to gather more information about what they are like?

Eventually, Jackie decided that one of the presents could be a book or a video.

c Discuss some of the ways a book and a video are similar, and some of the ways they are different.

Finally Jackie decided the present was a video. She had collected her evidence and used her model of a video to explain what she could see and feel about the present.

Scientific models

Scientists use models to help them think about how things work or behave. First they think about the evidence they have collected, and then they use a model that might explain it. You have met the particle model in this unit. Now try using it to explain the following three events.

(1) Feeling the cold

d Write a sentence, using the particle model, to explain what happened to the balloon in photo **C**.

e Use the particle model to predict what will happen to the balloon as it warms up again.

The air particles inside are moving quickly and hitting the sides of the balloon.

As the particles get colder they begin to move a lot slower. They get much closer together.

A A balloon was inflated with air.

B The balloon is dunked into liquid nitrogen. This is very cold indeed.

C The cold balloon is a lot smaller.

(2) Glass-blowing

The person in the photo is making a bottle. This is called glass-blowing. A ball of glass is heated until it is red-hot. When it is hot, the glass can be stretched or shaped. Once it is the right shape, the glass is left to cool.

f Is the hot glass like a liquid or a solid? Explain why you think this.

g Use the particle model to explain what happened to the ball of glass as it was heated until it was red-hot.

(3) Gassy problem

The gas that comes out of the gas tap is called methane. You usually think of methane as a gas, but there are some places where methane looks very different. The planet Uranus is so cold that it has liquid methane on its surface.

h Use your knowledge of the particle model to explain what would happen to the methane on Uranus if it got warmer.

Questions

1. Hydrogen and helium are both gases on Earth. The surface of Jupiter contains liquid hydrogen and helium. What does this tell you about the temperature on Jupiter?

2. Why do scientists use models like the particle model?

3. In windows that are hundreds of years old, the glass gradually flows downwards so that it is thicker at the bottom than the top. What does this tell you about glass? Does this evidence tell you that glass is a solid or a liquid?

Organically grown

Getting food

All animals and plants need food. Food gives them the energy they need to carry out their life processes. Plants make their own food by photosynthesis. Animals have to find their food. It is easy for people in the developed world to get food. We just go to the nearest supermarket.

a Make a list of the life processes.

b Describe what happens in photosynthesis.

As you go around most supermarkets you will see many different types of fruits and vegetables from all around the world. You can see bananas from the Caribbean, green beans from Africa, cheese from England and Holland and meat from Wales and New Zealand.

Some foods have labels. You may have noticed that some labels say 'organic' or 'organically grown', like the ones here.

A few years ago there were very few organic fruits and vegetables in supermarkets. Now you will see many different organic foods. **Organic** is a word used to describe food that has been grown without using manufactured chemicals.

Organic farming uses some farming methods that have been around for hundreds of years. Different crops are grown in the fields in different years. Natural fertilisers such as manure are used instead of manufactured fertilisers. These natural fertilisers do less damage around the farm, and they keep the soil fertile.

c Name one kind of product used on farms that are not organic.

d What do organic farmers use instead of this product?

Why people want organic food

More and more people are buying organic food. Some people want it because it is better for the environment. It does not damage wildlife because harmful chemicals are not used.

Some people want organic food because it is healthier. It does not contain any manufactured chemicals. There may be small amounts of these chemicals left behind in non-organic food.

Organically produced animals such as pigs are given good food so that they stay healthy. They are given more space to live in.

Disadvantages of organic food

If chemicals are not used, some of the crop may be spoiled by pests that eat it, or it may be damaged by diseases. This can make organic food more expensive to produce.

e Which do you think would produce more crop, a field on an organic farm or a field of the same size on a non-organic farm?

Non-organic farmers use wax to coat their fruits, and food dyes to make their food look nice. Organic farmers do not change the food like this, so organic food often does not look as good as non-organic food.

f Why are people prepared to pay more for organic food?

Questions

1. What is different about organic food?

2. Make a table to list the disadvantages and advantages of organic farming.

3. What you think will happen to the amount of organic food grown in the future?

4. Design a leaflet explaining why people might consider buying organic food.

What's in food?

What are nutrients?

Food contains many different substances. The useful substances that food contains are called **nutrients**. Look at the food label shown below.

NUTRITION		
TYPICAL COMPOSITION	A 30g serving with 125ml semi-skimmed milk provides	100g (3¹/₂oz) provide
Energy	718kJ/170kcal*	1560kJ/367kcal
Protein	6.3 g	7.3 g
Carbohydrate	31.1 g	82.7 g
of which sugars	8.9 g	8.9 g
Fat	2.2 g*	0.8 g
of which saturates	1.5 g	0.3 g
Fibre**	1.1 g	3.6 g
Sodium	0.4 g	1.1 g
VITAMINS/MINERALS		
Vitamin D	1.6µg (32% RDA)	5.0µg (100% RDA)
Thiamin	0.5mg (34% RDA)	1.4mg (100% RDA)
Riboflavin	0.7mg (44% RDA)	1.6mg (100% RDA)
Niacin	6.5mg (36% RDA)	18.0mg (100% RDA)
Vitamin B₆	0.7mg (34% RDA)	2.0mg (100% RDA)
Folic acid	127.5µg (63% RDA)	400.0µg (200% RDA)
Vitamin B₁₂	0.8µg (80% RDA)	1.0µg (100% RDA)
Pantothenic acid	2.2mg (37% RDA)	6.0mg (100% RDA)
Iron	4.3mg (30% RDA)	14.0mg (100% RDA)
RDA = Recommended Daily Allowance		
This pack contains approx 16 servings		
INFORMATION		

a What are the main types of nutrient listed in this food?

The main nutrients – carbohydrates, fats and protein

Carbohydrates give you energy. They are found in bread, potatoes, cakes and sweets. Sugar and starch are both carbohydrates.

Fats also give you energy. Fat insulates your body. Fats are found in butter, margarine, full fat milk and meat.

Proteins help your body to grow and repair itself. They are found in meat, fish, eggs, peas, beans and milk.

b Give two examples of foods that contain lots of carbohydrates.

c What function does protein have in your body?

Small amounts – vitamins and minerals

Vitamins are needed in very small amounts to keep the body healthy. Different vitamins have different jobs. If a vitamin is missing from someone's diet, it can cause a disease.

Vitamin A is found in carrots and helps to keep your skin and eyes healthy.

Vitamin C is found in fruit and green vegetables. Sailors on long voyages did not used to eat any fresh food. They did not eat enough vitamin C and they got the disease **scurvy**. Their gums bled and their teeth fell out. If they cut themselves, the skin did not heal.

Vitamin D is found in milk and butter. It is also made by your body in sunlight. Vitamin D gives you strong bones and teeth. If this vitamin is missing it can cause a disease called **rickets** where the bones are soft.

d Which vitamin prevents scurvy?

e Which vegetable provides lots of vitamin A?

Your body also needs **minerals** in small amounts. Different minerals have different functions.

Calcium is found in milk and cheese. You need calcium for healthy teeth and bones. **Iron** is found in liver and eggs and is used to make blood. If iron is missing from the diet it can cause **anaemia**. People with anaemia are pale and feel tired.

f Which mineral is needed for healthy bones and teeth?

Fibre and water

Fibre is also needed in your diet. Fibre is sometimes called **roughage** and it is found in cereals, fruit and vegetables. It helps food to keep moving through the gut. Fibre prevents you from becoming constipated and may reduce the risk of some types of cancer.

g Why is fibre good for you?

You take in **water** when you eat and drink. You would die in a few days without water. All the chemical reactions in your body take place in water.

Questions

1. Write out each nutrient along with the function it has in the body.

Nutrients	Functions
fat	provides energy
carbohydrate	provides energy and helps prevent the body losing heat
protein	needed in very small amounts to keep the body healthy
vitamins	for growth and repair

2. Explain the function of fibre in the diet. Which foods are high in fibre?

3. Write a list of all the foods you eat in a whole day. How could you improve your diet?

4. Write a rhyme to help you remember the major groups of nutrients. For example,

Very **F**it **P**eople **M**unch **C**arrots could stand for **V**itamins **F**at **P**rotein **M**inerals **C**arbohydrates

Did you know?
Your body loses about $2\frac{1}{2}$ litres of water a day, most of it as urine.

For your notes

Food contains useful substances called **nutrients**.

The main types of nutrient in food are **carbohydrates**, **fats**, **proteins**, **vitamins** and **minerals**.

Fibre and **water** are also needed for a healthy diet.

Balanced diet

Getting the balance right

Your body needs nutrients for energy and to keep you fit and healthy. A diet that has the right amounts of all the nutrients is called a **balanced diet**. A balanced diet gives you the right amounts of carbohydrates, fats, proteins, vitamins, minerals, fibre and water.

How much should we eat?

Government scientists tell us how much of each nutrient we should eat a day to give us a balanced diet. They set **recommended daily intakes (RDI)** or **recommended daily allowances (RDA)** for some of the nutrients and for the amount of energy in food. The picture shows us how much energy an adult man and woman need.

The amount of energy you need in your food depends on how much energy your body uses up every day. This depends on whether you are growing, how active you are and the size of your body. Men need more energy than women.

a What does RDI stand for?

b Why do different people need different amounts of energy?

Balancing the energy

A teenage boy uses about 12 500 kJ of energy every day, while a girl of the same age uses about 10 000 kJ. A person doing a very active job such as a builder uses a lot more energy than an office worker of the same age and sex.

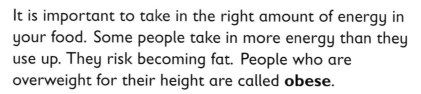

It is important to take in the right amount of energy in your food. Some people take in more energy than they use up. They risk becoming fat. People who are overweight for their height are called **obese**.

Some people do not eat enough food to give them energy for their body's needs and they lose weight. Obese people may eat less in order to lose weight.

You should always speak to your doctor before going on a diet. Sometimes people can suffer from eating disorders such as **anorexia nervosa**. They do not eat enough and they become very underweight. This disease can kill.

c Explain what can happen if you do not take in the correct amount of energy in your food.

Different diets

We have seen that different people need different amounts of energy every day. Some people also need different nutrients to stay healthy.

Pregnant women need to be careful what they eat and drink as it may affect the developing fetus.

Pregnant women may take folic acid. This helps prevent certain kinds of disability in the baby. Women also need extra nutrients in the last three months of pregnancy.

Sports people use a lot of energy and they need to take in energy very quickly. They often use drinks that contain a lot of sugars such as glucose that provide energy very quickly.

d Why do you think pregnant women need extra nutrients in the last three months of pregnancy?

e Why do sprinters take a lot of glucose?

People from different cultures eat different foods. This may be due to religion, tradition or simply what is available in the country. In many Asian countries such as China the main food is rice. In some countries in Europe, potatoes made up a large part of people's diets until recently, when rice and pasta became more popular.

In developed countries such as the UK the diet often contains too much fat and salt. A person who eats a high-fat diet is more likely to have a heart attack. A diet high in salt can increase the risk of having strokes. This kind of diet is often termed the 'Western diet'.

Questions

1. Use the following words to write a paragraph about balanced diets.

> **energy carbohydrates fats proteins minerals vitamins iron vitamin C water fibre pregnant diet**

2. Explain why a woman working in an office needs less energy than a man working on a building site.

3. In many developing countries people are now eating a more 'Western style' diet. What effect do you think this might have on their health?

For your notes

A diet that has the right amount of each nutrient is called a **balanced diet.**

It is important to balance the energy in your food with the energy your body uses.

The start

Food contains nutrients, but to get the nutrients into our bodies the food must be broken down into smaller molecules. This process is called **digestion**.

Digestion starts in the mouth where the food is broken up into smaller pieces by the teeth. The human mouth contains front teeth called **incisors** and back teeth called **molars**. Incisors are used for cutting food and molars for chewing. There are also **canine** teeth for piercing and tearing meat. Chopping up food in this way is a physical process.

a Sheep do not have canine teeth. Why do you think this is?

Down the tube

The **digestive system** is all the organs that take part in digestion. These are shown in the diagram opposite.

After the food leaves the mouth it passes through a tube called the **gut** which is 9 metres long. The first part of the tube is called the **gullet** or **oesophagus**. This links the mouth and stomach. It has muscular walls that push the food down. This is called **peristalsis**. Peristalsis is a bit like a tennis ball being pushed down an empty pair of tights.

Learn about

- The digestive system
- Absorption

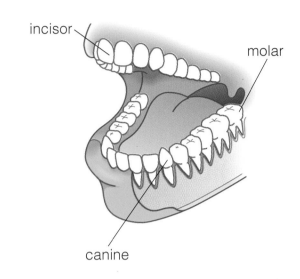

incisor
molar
canine

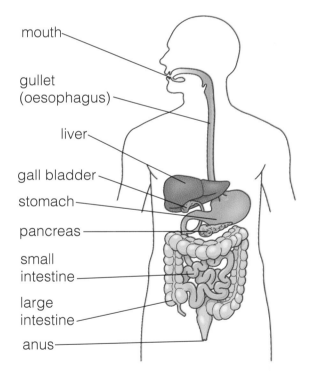

mouth
gullet (oesophagus)
liver
gall bladder
stomach
pancreas
small intestine
large intestine
anus

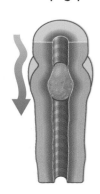
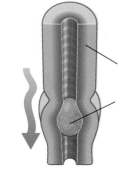

oesophagus

food pushed along

b Name the tube that links the mouth and the stomach.

In the **stomach** the food is churned up for a few hours by its muscular walls. Digestive juices are added. These contain **enzymes** and acid. Enzymes are made by the body to help break down the food. The acid in the stomach kills germs and makes the enzymes work at their best.

c What happens in the stomach?

After a few hours the food has become a runny liquid. This leaves the stomach and enters the **small intestine**. This is a long tube where three different liquids are added:

● pancreatic juice   ● bile

● intestinal juice.

These liquids contain enzymes that help to break down the different substances in food. Bile is alkaline so it neutralises the acid from the stomach.

An absorbing process

The digested food is now made up of small molecules. These pass through the lining of the small intestine into the blood. This process is called **absorption**.

The small intestine has millions of tiny finger-like structures called **villi** (singular **villus**) on its surface, as shown in the photo. The villi make the surface of the small intestine much larger. The large surface makes sure that the digested food is absorbed quickly.

d What gives the small intestine a large surface area?

e What happens to the digested food in the small intestine?

What's left?

Some undigested food, mainly fibre, is left in the small intestine. It is not absorbed into the blood in the small intestine because its molecules are too big. It passes into the **large intestine**. Here the waste food can be stored, and water is absorbed from it into the blood to be used by the body. Later the waste is pushed out of the body through the **anus**. This process is called **egestion**. The waste that is egested is called **faeces**.

Questions

1. Copy and complete the following sentences, choosing from the words below.

> stomach mouth small intestine teeth anus
> pancreas liver oesophagus large intestine

a Water is absorbed in the …
b Acidic conditions are found in the …
c Food is absorbed in the …
d Food is egested through the …

2. Explain what these words mean:
a egestion   **b** peristalsis

3. Draw a flow chart to show the parts of the digestive system that food passes through in order, starting at the mouth.

For your notes

Digestion takes place in the **digestive system**.

This consists of the **mouth, oesophagus, stomach, small intestine, large intestine** and **anus**.

Small molecules of digested food are **absorbed** into the blood.

Enzymes

Total breakdown

In the mouth, the teeth help break up the food into smaller pieces. This mechanical breakdown of the food is a physical process.

When we **digest** food, the small pieces of food are broken down even further into substances with small molecules. Only small molecules can be absorbed through the lining of the small intestine into the blood. Large molecules cannot pass through the lining. Breaking down food into smaller molecules is a chemical process.

a What sort of molecules can pass through the lining of the small intestine?

Enzymes – chemical breakers

In digestion, chemicals called **enzymes** help to break the larger molecules into smaller molecules. Enzymes make the digestion of food happen more quickly. Without enzymes it could take a few days instead of a few hours to break down some foods. Enzymes for digesting food are found in the mouth, stomach and small intestine.

b i What are enzymes?
 ii Why are enzymes important in digestion?

Each enzyme helps break down a different type of nutrient. Some break down carbohydrates, some break down proteins and others break down fats.

There are large carbohydrate molecules such as starch in foods like bread, rice and pasta. These are broken down into small **glucose** molecules.

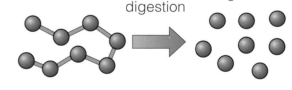

starch · digestion · glucose

c What happens to starch when it is digested?

Naming enzymes

Enzymes in digestion are normally named after the substances they break down. The name of an enzyme ends in the letters '-ase'. For example, protease breaks down proteins.

d Which of the following are enzymes?

> fat carbohydrate protease vitamin amylase glucose starch

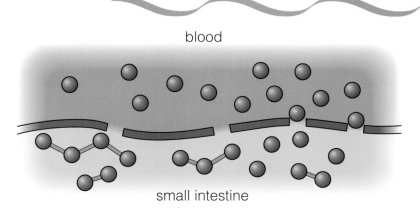

blood

small intestine

More about absorption

Look at the diagram opposite. Small molecules such as glucose can pass through the wall of the gut. They pass into the blood to be carried away to the parts of the body where they are needed. Large starch molecules need to be broken down to smaller glucose molecules before they can be absorbed.

Did you know?

Some washing powders are described as 'biological', and others are 'non-biological'. **Biological washing powders** contain enzymes such as protease that help to clean dirty clothes.

e The idea of small fish and fishing nets is a model to help you imagine how absorption happens. Look at the picture on the left. Which part of the model represents:
   i large molecules such as starch?
   ii small molecules such as glucose?
   iii the wall of the small intestine?

Some substances in food such as minerals and vitamins are small enough to go straight through the gut wall. Other substances such as parts of sweetcorn cannot be broken down as there are no enzymes to do it.

Questions

1. Copy and complete these sentences.

The breakdown of food is called _____. It is both a chemical and a _____ process. Substances called _____ help the chemical process happen. They make the breakdown of food _____. When starch is broken down completely, _____ molecules are formed.

2. Explain why some substances can pass through the gut lining without being broken down.

3. Design a poster to show how food is broken down.

For your notes

Digestion uses physical and chemical processes to break down food into smaller molecules.

Enzymes speed up the breakdown of food.

Different enzymes work on different nutrients.

Food for energy

Food and energy

Food gives you energy. Carbohydrates, fats and proteins provide your body with the energy you need to stay healthy. The energy is used for many things such as working your muscles and organs, growing and repairing cells and keeping your body temperature constant. Your food is the fuel that keeps you going.

a What nutrients are the main sources of energy?

Fuels and respiration

When a fuel such as petrol or natural gas is burned, chemical energy is transferred to light energy and heat energy. The fuel reacts with oxygen to produce carbon dioxide and water, and energy is released. Your body uses a similar reaction to get the energy from food. It is called **respiration**.

The fuel used in respiration is glucose. The glucose comes from the digestion of food. The oxygen for respiration comes from the air you breathe in. Carbon dioxide, water and energy are produced by respiration. The waste carbon dioxide and water are added to the air you breathe out.

Respiration can be shown in a word equation:

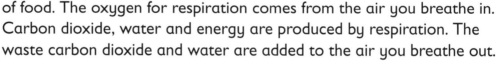

glucose + oxygen → carbon dioxide + water

energy given out

b What are the reactants in respiration?

c What are the products in respiration?

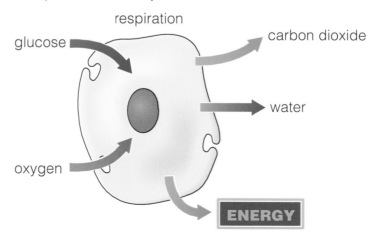

respiration

glucose

carbon dioxide

water

oxygen

ENERGY

Where does respiration happen?

Respiration takes place inside all living cells. It happens in small structures called **mitochondria** inside the cells.

d Where does respiration happen in your body?

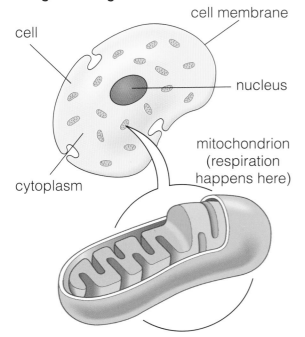

cell

cell membrane

nucleus

cytoplasm

mitochondrion (respiration happens here)

Transport for respiration

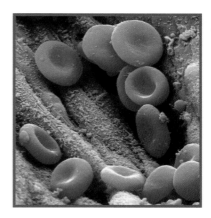

In larger organisms the oxygen and glucose needed for respiration are transported to the cells by the blood. Look at the photo of red blood cells. Oxygen travels attached to a special chemical called **haemoglobin** in red blood cells. Glucose is dissolved in the blood. Oxygen and glucose can pass from the blood to nearby cells where they are needed.

e How is oxygen taken around the body?

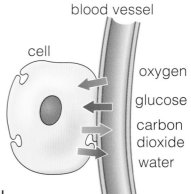

blood vessel

cell

oxygen

glucose

carbon dioxide

water

The waste products from respiration are carbon dioxide and water. The water may be used in the cell, or it may pass into the blood to be taken away. Carbon dioxide is taken away dissolved in the blood.

Questions

1. Copy and complete these sentences.

Respiration is the process by which living things get their _____. It takes place inside living _____ and can be summarised in the word equation:

_____ + oxygen → carbon dioxide + _____

energy given out

2. What is the energy from respiration used for?

3. Describe the journey of a molecule of oxygen from being breathed in to being used in respiration.

For your notes

Respiration is the process by which living things get energy from food.

Respiration can be summarised by the equation:

glucose + oxygen → carbon dioxide + water

energy given out

Chewing it over

Digestion of starch

Wendy took a bite of her baguette. She thought, 'The bigger the bite, the more starch there is to be digested, and the longer it takes ...'.

Wendy wanted to find out whether adding more of an enzyme to starch speeds up digestion. Starch is broken down into glucose by an enzyme called salivary amylase.

She used the same amount of starch each time, but added different amounts of the enzyme. She used iodine indicator to show when the starch had disappeared. She timed how long it took for the starch to disappear each time. When the starch had disappeared, she knew it had all been digested.

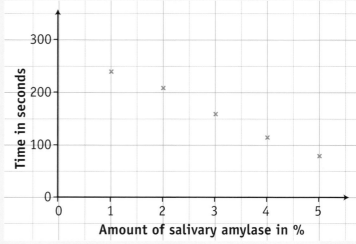

The input variable (the thing she changed) was the amount of enzyme. The outcome variable (the thing she measured) was the time taken to digest the starch. Her results are shown in the table.

Amount (concentration) of salivary amylase in %	Time taken to digest all the starch in seconds
1	240
2	210
3	160
4	115
5	80

Wendy wanted to see if there was a pattern in her results. She drew a line graph. She put the input variable on the *x*-axis, along the bottom. She put the outcome variable on the *y*-axis, up the side. She plotted her results on the graph.

a Copy Wendy's graph. Try to draw a straight line on the graph to show the pattern of her results.

b Can you draw a straight line through all her crosses?

Lines of best fit

In many experiments, you cannot draw a line that passes through all the points. You have to draw a line that fits most of them. This is called the **line of best fit**.

Wendy and her friends were discussing why the graph may not go through all the points in an experiment.

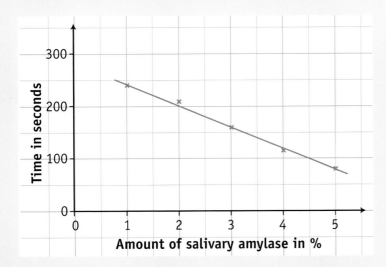

We forgot to start the timer.

Science experiments are always a bit inaccurate.

We forgot to watch the clock, and we took some readings a bit late.

The timer was not accurate enough.

We did the experiment all wrong.

Maybe some wells in the spotting tile were dirty.

c Which of their ideas above might explain why the graph did not go through all the points?

This is what Wendy's graph looked like when she had drawn in a line of best fit.

Time in seconds (y-axis, 0 to 300)
Amount of salivary amylase in % (x-axis, 0 to 5)

d What pattern do you see in the results?

e Describe the relationship between the input variable and the outcome variable.

f Why do you think that some of the points do not fit the pattern?

Interpreting graphs

Drawing a line of best fit helps you see the relationship shown by the graph. Once you have a line of best fit, you can read other results off it to make predictions.

Wendy can now use this graph to predict how long it would probably take for other amounts of amylase to digest starch. She drew a line up to the graph from 1.5% on the x-axis, and read off the time on the y-axis. The diagram shows this.

g Why do you think she would want to do this?

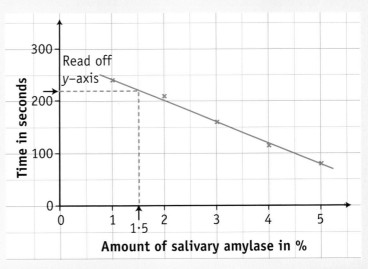

Read off y–axis

Time in seconds (y-axis, 0 to 300)
1·5
Amount of salivary amylase in % (x-axis, 0 to 5)

Questions

1. Why do we use lines of best fit?

2. Sometimes the results do not all fit the pattern of the graph. Think about any experiments you have carried out in the past where the results where not what you expected. Why did this happen?

The right fuel for the job

What makes a good fuel?

John, Clarissa and Dermont are discussing what makes an ideal fuel.

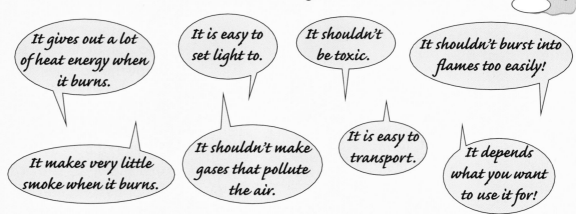

It gives out a lot of heat energy when it burns.

It is easy to set light to.

It shouldn't be toxic.

It shouldn't burst into flames too easily!

It makes very little smoke when it burns.

It shouldn't make gases that pollute the air.

It is easy to transport.

It depends what you want to use it for!

a Pick one of petrol, coal and natural gas. Is it an ideal fuel?

Keep the home fires burning

Our homes used to be heated using fires. In Britain we use wood, coal or 'smokeless' fuel for our fires.

b What substance in the air is involved in all burning reactions?

c 'Smokeless' fuel is mainly carbon. Copy and complete this word equation for burning carbon.

carbon + oxygen → _____

d Copy and complete this energy transfer diagram for a wood fire.

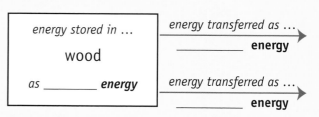

energy stored in …
wood
as _____ **energy**

energy transferred as …
_____ **energy**

energy transferred as …
_____ **energy**

Other people around the world use different fuels. Inuits, who live in a frozen wasteland, use blubber. Blubber is the layer of fat found under the skins of seals. The Bedouin people live in the desert. They use camel dung for a fuel.

e Why do neither the Inuits nor the Bedouin use wood as a fuel?

f Where did the energy in the camel dung come from? Draw an energy transfer diagram to explain your answer.

Fuels for vehicles

When a fuel burns, it reacts with oxygen from the air. In space there is no air, so you have to take the oxygen with you.

Questions

1. The table below gives you information about six different fuels.
   Photos **A** to **F** show six different vehicles.
   a Pair up each vehicle with its fuel. Write down the pairs.
   b Make a list of reasons for each choice, so you are ready to join in a discussion.

Fuel	Reacts with	Notes
Nitromethane and methanol	Oxygen from the air	The energy is released in a sudden burst. The fuel burns very quickly.
Coal	Oxygen from the air	The fuel burns steadily.
Liquid hydrogen	Liquid oxygen	Liquid hydrogen and oxygen are expensive. They are kept in huge insulated tanks and pumped into the fuel tank when needed.
Petrol	Oxygen from the air	Petrol is available from petrol stations. It is easily pumped.
Diesel	Oxygen from the air	Diesel is available from petrol stations. It is cheaper than petrol. Diesel engines give poorer performance than petrol engines.
Kerosene	Oxygen from the air	Kerosene is more expensive than petrol. It gives out more energy than petrol.

What are fossil fuels?

We find **coal**, **oil** and **natural gas** inside rocks. Coal, oil and natural gas are fuels because they give out energy when they are burned. They are called **fossil fuels** because they formed from animals and plants that lived millions of years ago. A fossil is the dead remains of an animal or plant found in rock.

Why are fossil fuels important?

Fuels for vehicles, like petrol or diesel, are made from crude oil. We burn oil, coal or natural gas to heat our homes. We use a lot of electricity. This electricity comes from a power station. Most power stations burn coal, oil or natural gas to make the electricity.

Crude oil is a very useful raw material. We make plastics and many other materials from crude oil. All the objects in the photo were made from crude oil.

a Explain how fossil fuels help you to:
  i travel by car   **ii** play football.

Making coal

1. Millions of years ago, plants trapped the energy in sunlight, made food and grew.

2. When the plants died they were buried. The plants did not rot. This was because they were away from the air. Oxygen in the air helps rotting.

3. More layers of mud and sediment put the plants under a lot of pressure. The plants were heated to about 100 °C.

4. The heat and pressure turned the plants into coal. They turned the mud and sediment into rocks. This took millions of years.

b Why did dead plants turn into coal rather than rotting away?

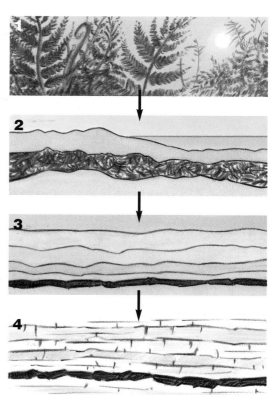

Making oil and natural gas

Oil and natural gas were made from animals rather than plants. Many millions of years ago the sea was full of tiny animals. When these animals died they sank to the bottom of the sea. There was no oxygen at the bottom of the sea, so they did not rot.

The dead sea animals were buried under layer after layer of sediment. The layers of sediment were heavy, so the dead sea animals were under pressure. They were heated to about 100°C. The dead sea animals changed into crude oil and natural gas, while the sediment turned into rock. This took many millions of years.

c The tiny sea animals ate plants. How did these plants make their food?

d Look at the energy transfer below.
  i What is **A**?
  ii What types of energy are **B** and **C**?

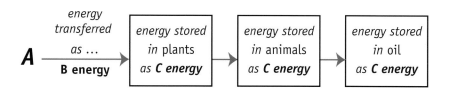

What's in fossil fuels?

Many of the substances in fossil fuels are hydrocarbons. Hydrocarbons contain only carbon and hydrogen atoms.

Natural gas contains a lot of **methane**. Methane is a hydrocarbon. Each methane molecule has one carbon atom and four hydrogen atoms.

e Which of the substances **A** to **E** are hydrocarbons?

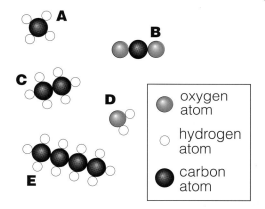

Questions

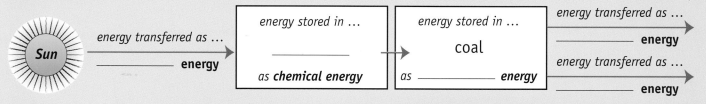

1. Copy and complete this energy transfer diagram. It shows how energy from the Sun was trapped in coal. This energy is released when the coal is burned.

2. Draw and label a series of diagrams showing how oil was made. Include all the information at the top of this page. (You may like to use the diagram about coal as a pattern.)

For your notes

The energy in fossil fuels came from the Sun.

Fossil fuels:

- include coal, crude oil and natural gas
- give us the energy we need and are important raw materials
- were made from buried animals and plants. This took many millions of years.

Releasing the energy

Natural gas is mostly methane. Burning natural gas makes carbon dioxide and water, and gives out a lot of heat energy. A small amount of energy is also given out as light energy.

a Copy and complete this word equation for the burning of methane.

methane + oxygen → _____ + _____

Coal contains both carbon and sulfur. The carbon and sulfur react with oxygen when the coal burns.

carbon + oxygen → carbon dioxide

sulfur + oxygen → sulfur dioxide

Not all the carbon in the coal burns. Little bits of carbon are left. These make smoke.

b Copy and complete this energy transfer diagram for burning coal.

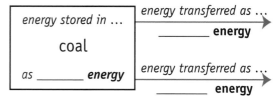

energy stored in ...
coal
as _____ **energy**

energy transferred as ...
_____ **energy**

energy transferred as ...
_____ **energy**

Oil is different. Crude oil is a thick, sticky liquid that will not burn. The crude oil has to be distilled. This separates the crude oil into many useful fuels, including petrol and diesel.

c What are petrol and diesel used for?

Global warming

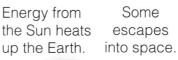

Burning fossil fuels makes carbon dioxide. Adding more carbon dioxide to the air will increase the greenhouse effect. More of the energy from the Sun will get trapped in the Earth's atmosphere. The Earth will become hotter. This is called **global warming**.

A hotter Earth will be different. Some of the ice at the North and South Poles will melt. The water in the seas will heat up and expand. This will make the sea level rise, and some land will be flooded. The weather will change. Some places will get more rain, others will get less rain.

d How will the Earth change if it heats up?

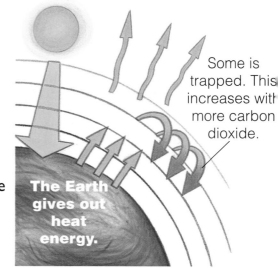

Energy from the Sun heats up the Earth.   Some escapes into space.

Some is trapped. This increases with more carbon dioxide.

The Earth gives out heat energy.

Air pollution

Burning coal makes sulfur dioxide. Sulfur dioxide dissolves in the water in the air and causes acid rain. We try to remove sulfur dioxide from smoke before it goes into the air. We put chemical **scrubbers** in chimneys to remove the sulfur dioxide. These chemical scrubbers contain an alkali. The alkali reacts with the acid, making it neutral.

e Look at the table. Each solution has been tested with universal indicator. Which solution would be useful as chemical scrubbers to remove the sulfur dioxide from smoke? Explain your choice.

Solution	pH
Sodium chloride	7
Sodium chlorate	3
Sodium hydroxide	14

Cars and lorries burn petrol and diesel. This produces substances that pollute the air. Cars and lorries give out smoke, nitrogen oxides, carbon monoxide, unburned hydrocarbons and carbon dioxide. Places with lots of cars end up with very polluted air. This can cause health problems.

We can reduce the air pollution by fitting cars with **catalytic converters**. Catalytic converters change nitrogen oxides into nitrogen and carbon monoxide into carbon dioxide. Nitrogen causes no pollution and carbon dioxide causes no local pollution (although it does cause global warming). Car sharing and using public transport would decrease the number of cars on the roads. This would also reduce air pollution.

f Cars give out waste gases. What substances are in the waste gases of:
   i a car without a catalytic converter?
   ii a car with a catalytic converter?

Questions

1. Draw an energy transfer diagram for petrol burning.

2. Why does burning fossil fuels increase the greenhouse effect?

3. Why does burning coal increase acid rain?

4. Global warming may cause a rise in sea level. What will happen if the sea level rises?

5. In Athens you can only drive your car on Mondays, Wednesdays and Fridays or Tuesdays, Thursdays and Saturdays.
   a How does this decrease air pollution?
   b Do you think it is a good idea?

For your notes

Heat energy is given out when fossil fuels are burned.

Carbon dioxide is made when fossil fuels are burned.

Increased amounts of carbon dioxide in the air may cause **global warming**.

Burning coal makes sulfur dioxide, which causes acid rain.

Electricity from fossil fuels

Inside a power station

Our electricity is made in power stations. Most of our power stations use fossil fuels. The fossil fuels are burned, and the energy given out is transferred to electricity.

Water is heated in the boiler, and turned into steam. The steam rushes out of the boiler and into the **turbine**, like steam rushing out of a kettle. The steam turns the blades of the turbine.

The spinning turbine turns the **generator**. When the generator turns it makes electricity.

Learn about

➤ How fossil fuels are used to make electricity

(a) What turns the turbine?

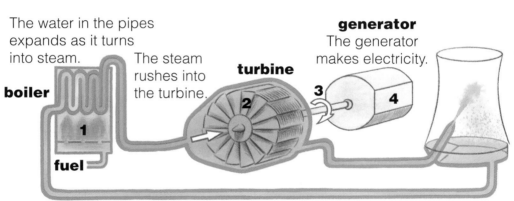

The water in the pipes expands as it turns into steam.

The steam rushes into the turbine.

boiler

1

fuel

turbine

2

generator
The generator makes electricity.

3   4

The steam is condensed back into water in the cooling towers, then returned to the boiler.

Transferring the energy

1. The fossil fuels are burned, giving out heat energy (**thermal** energy). This heats water and turns it into steam.

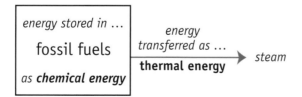

energy stored in ...
fossil fuels
as **chemical energy**
energy transferred as ...
thermal energy
→ steam

2. Movement energy (**kinetic** energy) is transferred to the turbine by the steam.

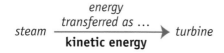

steam
energy transferred as ...
kinetic energy
→ turbine

(b) What carries the energy from the boiler to the turbine?

3. Movement energy (kinetic energy) is transferred from the turbine to the generator.

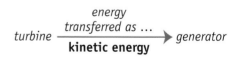

turbine
energy transferred as ...
kinetic energy
→ generator

4. The generator takes in kinetic energy and gives out electrical energy.

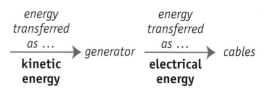

energy transferred as ...
kinetic energy
→ generator
energy transferred as ...
electrical energy
→ cables

(c) What part of the power station takes in kinetic (movement) energy and gives out electrical energy?

Wasted energy

Only a small amount of the energy released from the burning fuel ends up as electrical energy. Burning the fuel heats up the air as well as the water. Not all the energy in the steam is transferred to the turbine. There is friction in the turbine and the generator. The friction means that some of the energy heats up the machines and is wasted.

d Does the 'wasted' energy end up as electrical energy or thermal (heat) energy?

The future

Fossil fuels are going to run out. They are **non-renewable** energy resources. The fossil fuels took many millions of years to form. They are not being replaced as we use them.

Scientists think we will run out of oil in about 2030, natural gas in about 2050 and coal in about 2230. That means there will be no petrol after 2030. It means that we will have to find new energy resources for our power stations. At the moment, 90% of our energy comes from fossil fuels. We need to find other ways to get the energy we need. These are called **alternative** energy resources.

e Look at the bar chart. How many years will it be before we use up all the: **i** coal?   **ii** natural gas?   **iii** oil?

f We cannot be sure that all the oil will be used up by 2030. Why not? Give two reasons.

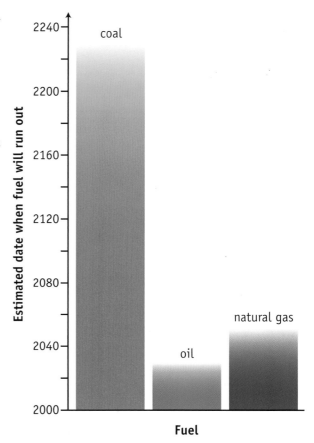

Questions

1. Why are coal, oil and natural gas **non-renewable** energy resources?

2. Why will there probably be no natural gas or oil in 60 years' time?

3. In a power station, what type of energy is passed on by:
   i the burning fuel?   **ii** the turbine?   **iii** the generator?

4. Use the information on these two pages to draw an energy transfer diagram that shows all the useful energy transfers in a power station. You will need a large piece of paper.

For your notes

Power stations change the chemical energy stored in fuels into electrical energy.

Only a small part of the energy in the fuel ends up as electrical energy.

Non-renewable energy resources (such as fossil fuels) are not replaced as fast as we use them.

Turning the turbine

Biomass

Methane is a fuel. We find methane in natural gas, but methane can also be made from rotting material. The tank in the photo contains farm waste. Methane is made from it as it rots. This methane is an example of **biomass**. Biomass is material from plants and animals. It can be used as an energy resource. Wood is another example of biomass.

The energy in the biomass comes from the Sun. The plants trap the Sun's energy to make their food and grow. The animals eat plants, or other animals that ate plants.

Wood, methane and other biomass fuels are **renewable** sources of energy. A tree only takes 10–15 years to grow. We produce a lot of rubbish that can be rotted to make methane. We can replace the biomass as we use it.

The biomass burns in the boiler of a power station. Burning gives out thermal energy that heats water and turns it into steam. The steam turns the turbine, which turns the generator and makes electricity.

Learn about

➤ Alternative energy resources

a Explain why wood is a renewable energy source, while coal is not.

Solar energy

Sunlight can turn water into steam. There is a lot of thermal energy in sunlight – you can burn paper using a magnifying glass! **Solar furnaces** are huge, curved mirrors that concentrate sunlight like a magnifying glass. Water is heated by the sunlight and turned into steam. The steam then turns the turbine.

The Sun shines every day, although clouds sometimes cover it. **Solar energy** is a renewable energy resource.

b The weather is often cloudy in Britain and the sunlight is not as hot as in some other countries.
  i We do not build solar furnaces in Britain. Why not?
  ii Suggest a country where people would build solar furnaces.

Wind energy

Wind turbines are turned by **wind energy**. The turbine turns the generator, making electricity.

$$\text{Sun} \xrightarrow[\textbf{thermal energy}]{\textit{energy transferred as} \ldots} \text{air} \xrightarrow[\textbf{kinetic energy}]{\textit{energy transferred as} \ldots} \text{turbine}$$

The Sun makes the winds. Thermal energy from the Sun heats the air. The air moves and there is wind. The Sun heats the air every day, so wind is a renewable energy resource.

c Why is wind a renewable energy resource?

Waves

Wave energy can also turn turbines. Look at the diagram. The wave pushes the water up. The water then pushes the air through the turbine. The turbine spins the generator, making electricity.

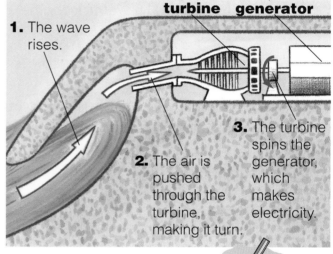

turbine   generator

1. The wave rises.

2. The air is pushed through the turbine, making it turn.

3. The turbine spins the generator, which makes electricity.

Waves are made by wind passing over the water. Winds are made by the Sun heating the air. This means that the energy in the waves comes from the Sun. This makes waves a renewable energy resource.

d What makes the waves?

e Are waves are renewable or non-renewable energy resource? Explain your answer.

Questions

1. Copy and complete this energy transfer diagram for a solar furnace.

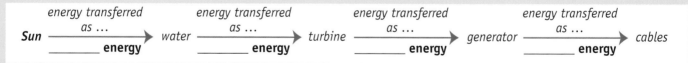

$$\text{Sun} \xrightarrow[\text{_____ energy}]{\textit{energy transferred as} \ldots} \text{water} \xrightarrow[\text{_____ energy}]{\textit{energy transferred as} \ldots} \text{turbine} \xrightarrow[\text{_____ energy}]{\textit{energy transferred as} \ldots} \text{generator} \xrightarrow[\text{_____ energy}]{\textit{energy transferred as} \ldots} \text{cables}$$

2. Biomass, solar energy, wind and waves are renewable energy resources. Coal, oil and natural gas are non-renewable energy resources.

   a What is the difference between a renewable energy resource and a non-renewable energy resource?

   b Why is it important to develop renewable energy resources?

For your notes

Biomass, solar power, wind and **waves:**
- are energy resources
- can be used to generate electricity
- are renewable
- get their energy from the Sun.

Renewable energy resources are replaced as we use them.

More turbines turning

Hydroelectric power

We use falling water to generate electricity. The water falls through the turbine, turning it. The turbine then turns the generator. This is called **hydroelectric** power.

Waterfalls can turn turbines. At Niagara Falls, shown in this photo, some of the water falls through turbines.

We can also build dams to make falling water. The second photo shows the Hoover Dam. The lake was made when the dam was built. The water from the lake falls through turbines inside the dam, making electricity.

The water in rivers comes from rain. The water in the rain has been lifted up when water was evaporated by the Sun. Water is evaporated each day, so falling water is a renewable energy resource.

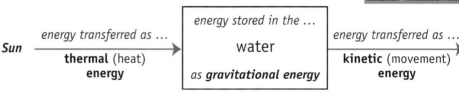

Sun $\xrightarrow[\textbf{thermal (heat) energy}]{\textit{energy transferred as ...}}$ | energy stored in the ... **water** as ***gravitational energy*** | $\xrightarrow[\textbf{kinetic (movement) energy}]{\textit{energy transferred as ...}}$ *turbine*

a Energy is needed for water to get up behind the dam. Where does this energy come from?

Tides

Tides lift water up. If the water is trapped, it can fall through a turbine, making electricity. The photo shows the dam across the Rance River in Brittany, France. The high tide pushes the water through the dam. The dam is then closed, trapping the water as the tide goes out. The trapped water then falls through the turbines.

Tides are not caused by thermal energy from the Sun. They are caused by gravity. The Moon and the Sun pull on the Earth, moving the water in the oceans. This pull is continuous, so tides are a renewable energy resource.

b Why is falling water a renewable energy resource?

c Where does the energy come from to lift up the water during a high tide?

Nuclear and geothermal energy

Some elements are **radioactive**. Their atoms break down, giving out lots of energy. At a **nuclear** power station, like the one shown in the photo opposite, this energy is used to heat water and turn it into steam. The steam then turns the turbine.

The inside of the Earth is hot. This is partly because the Earth contains radioactive elements. Their atoms break down, giving out energy that heats the rocks. In some places, these hot rocks are close to the surface. **Geothermal** power stations, like the one in the photo below, use this thermal energy to make electricity. Cold water is pumped down to the hot rocks and turns into steam. The steam turns a turbine, making electricity.

Nuclear and geothermal energy are not renewable, because the radioactive atoms are used up when they break down.

d Where does the energy come from to heat the water in a nuclear or geothermal power station?

Questions

1. Make a list of all the energy resources you have learned about. Look at pages 78–87 to help you.

2. Divide the energy resources into two groups, 'renewable' and 'non-renewable'. Make a table showing these groups.

Renewable	Non-renewable

3. Divide the energy resources into two new groups, 'get their energy from the Sun' and 'get their energy from radioactive elements or gravity'. Make a table showing these two groups.

Energy from the Sun	Energy not from the Sun

For your notes

Falling water is a renewable energy resource that can be used to generate electricity. This is called **hydroelectric power**.

The energy in falling river water comes from the Sun.

Tides can be used to make electricity. Tides are caused by gravity, not thermal energy from the Sun.

Nuclear and **geothermal** power are two other energy resources.

Getting around

Life without oil

We often travel by car or bus. The food and clothes we buy are transported by road, sea or air. Cars, ships and planes all need fuel, and those fuels are made from oil. But the oil runs out in 2030.

Conserving energy

We can try to make the oil last longer. We can make cars with smaller engines. Smaller engines burn less petrol and give us more miles to the gallon. However, we are going to run out of oil one day.

a Why are cars with small engines a good idea?

Alternative fuels

Brazil has very little oil. However, Brazil grows a lot of sugar. The Brazilians decided to make a fuel from sugar. They made the sugar into ethanol. They burned ethanol in their cars rather than petrol.

b Copy and complete this word equation for the burning of ethanol.

ethanol + _____ → carbon dioxide + water

Hydrogen may be a fuel for the future. Hydrogen is a very clean fuel because it only makes water when it burns. However, hydrogen is a gas so it is hard to carry around in a fuel tank. Also, hydrogen can explode when it is mixed with oxygen.

c Copy and complete this word equation for the burning of hydrogen.

hydrogen + oxygen → _____

d Why is hydrogen a cleaner fuel than ethanol?

Batteries

Another alternative to petrol is electric cars powered by **batteries**. We have had electric cars for years. Milk floats are powered by batteries. However, electric cars have never caught on.

Batteries were very heavy and only gave enough energy to travel short distances slowly. This energy transfer diagram shows what happens in an electric car.

energy stored in the ...
batteries
as **chemical energy**

energy transferred as ...
electrical energy

motor

energy transferred as ...
kinetic energy

Modern electric cars are more attractive than milk floats. Batteries now weigh less and can store more energy. The very best electric cars can match the speed of a petrol car. They can travel long distances before the batteries need

charging. However, these cars are very expensive. The batteries still take up a lot of room, often the whole of the boot or the whole of the back seat.

e What type of energy is stored in a battery?

f What type of energy is given out by a battery?

g The motor of an electric car takes in electrical energy. What type of energy does it give out?

Using electric cars would save fossil fuels because the cars do not burn petrol or diesel. However, the batteries in an electric car need charging every day. The electricity used to charge the batteries is made in a power station.

h If oil ran out, what energy resources could be used to make the electricity to charge the car's batteries?

Solar powered cars

Solar cells can be used to make electricity. Sunlight falls on the solar cell and it makes electricity. The Solar Challenge is a race across Australia for cars powered by solar cells.

The cars are not very practical. Look at the photo below of a car in the Solar Challenge. The car needs a large top surface. A lot of the top surface has to be covered with solar cells, which are very expensive. The car cannot carry much weight, just the driver. The car needs a lot of sunlight. That is why the race is held in Australia.

Questions

1. Copy and complete this energy transfer diagram for a solar cell.

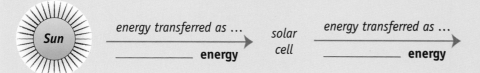

2. Why have battery cars failed to catch on?

3. Could you use a solar powered car, like the ones used in the Solar Challenge, as a family car in Britain? Give as many reasons as you can for you answer.

4. What are the advantages and disadvantages of hydrogen as a fuel?

For your notes

Batteries store chemical energy and convert it into electrical energy.

Solar cells convert light energy into electrical energy.

How many?

Counting wild animals

Some scientists wanted to know how many snails were living in a meadow. They **sampled** the snails. The flow chart shows how they did this. From their samples they **estimated** the number of snails in the meadow (the population).

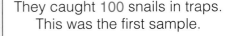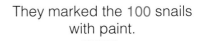

Snails painted = 100

Painted snails caught again = 10

'Painted snails caught again':'all snails painted'
= **10:100 = 1:10**

This means there are always **10** snails out there for every **1** snail caught.

So when they caught 50 snails, there were 50 × 10 = 500 snails in the meadow. The population of snails was 500.

You can write it like this: **10:100 = 1:10 = 50:?**   **? = 500**

They caught 100 snails in traps. This was the first sample.	
They marked the 100 snails with paint.	
They released the snails.	
A week later they took a second sample of 50 snails.	
They counted the snails in this sample with paint on their shells. There were 10.	

a How many snails were marked with paint?

b How many of these snails were caught again (recaptured)?

c What was the ratio of 'painted snails recaptured':'all snails painted'?

d What was the size of the second sample of snails?

e What was the ratio of 'size of second sample':'population'?

f How many snails were there in the meadow?

Studying pollution

A group of scientists went to a country where many new coal-fired power stations were being built. They studied two places where new power stations were being built (site 2 and site 4). They studied two places with no power station (site 1 and site 3).

All the power stations were built by lakes, because a power station needs lots of water. The scientists decided to study pollution by looking at living things. They studied a type of fish living in the lakes.

They caught 500 fish.

⬇

They put paint on each fish.

⬇

They released the fish.

⬇

One month later they took a second sample of 100 fish.

⬇

They counted the number of fish with paint.

⬇

They used ratios to estimate the population of fish.

The scientists sampled the fish at each site. The flow chart shows what they did. They repeated this every two years for ten years. They used different paint each time.

Look at the table.

g Which site had a power station built in:
   i 1989?   **ii** 1991?

h Copy the table and work out the populations for sites 1 and 2.

i Make a bar chart for each site. Set each bar chart out as shown.

j Look at the information for site 2 and site 4. Did building the power stations affect the populations of fish?

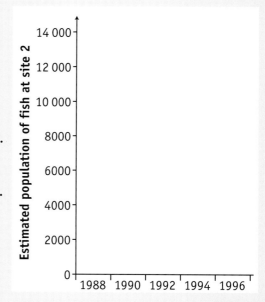

Code: fish marked with paint = 500   number of painted fish caught again
   sample size   population (what you need to work out)

☐ without power station   ▨ with power station

Site	1988	1990	1992	1994	1996
1	5 5:500 = 1:100 = 100:? ? = 10000	5	5	5	5
2	5 5:500 = 1:100 = 100:? ? = 10000	5	25 25:500 = 1:20 = 100:? ? = 2000	50	50
3	6 6:500 = 1:83.3 = 100:? ? = 8330	5 5:500 = 1:100 = 100:? ? = 10000	7 7:500 = 1:71.3 = 100:? ? = 7130	6 6:500 = 1:83 = 100:? ? = 8330	4 4:500 = 1:125 = 100:? ? = 12500
4	5 5:500 = 1:100 = 100:? ? = 10000	23 23:500 = 1:21.7 = 100:? ? = 2170	36 36:500 = 1:13.9 = 100:? ? = 1390	48 48:500 = 1:10.4 = 100:? ? = 1040	39 39:500 = 1:12.8 = 100:? ? = 1280

Questions

Think about the scientists' pollution research.

1. Why did the scientists study two sites without power stations?

2. Suggest two things *other than pollution* that could change the population of fish.

Earth detectives

Rocks

7.1

Setting the scene

The fossil finder

Mary Anning is often said to be the greatest fossil hunter ever. She was born in Lyme Regis, Dorset in 1799. When she was 11, her father died. This left the family very poor.

To make money for her family, Mary began to collect fossils from the local beach. She would then sell them to wealthy collectors and museums. Fossil hunting was a dangerous business. She had to walk and wade under crumbling cliffs at low tide.

Mary Anning.

Mary became well known as a fossil hunter and she made some very important discoveries. She found the first specimen of an *Ichthyosaurus* in 1821 and the first nearly complete skeleton of a *Plesiosaurus* in 1823. She found many other types of dinosaur as well.

> **Did you know?**
> The word 'dinosaur' means 'terrible lizard'.

Ichthyosaurus.

Plesiosaurus.

What are fossils?

Fossils are any parts of animals or plants that are preserved in rocks. Fossils are very important because they can tell us about organisms that lived millions of years ago. Much of our knowledge of the Earth's past comes from fossils. Being a geologist is a bit like being a detective.

Bones, shells and teeth are the best known fossils. But fossils can also be found of many other things, such as footprints, tiny seeds and animal dung.

a What is the name for scientists who study the Earth and rocks?

b What is a fossil?

c What sorts of things can become fossilised?

> **Did you know?**
> People who study rocks and the Earth are called **geologists**.

92

Rock history

Some fossils are found on the surface, while others are hidden under a layer of earth. They can tell us the story of events on the Earth thousands or millions of years ago. Time so long ago is called **geological time**.

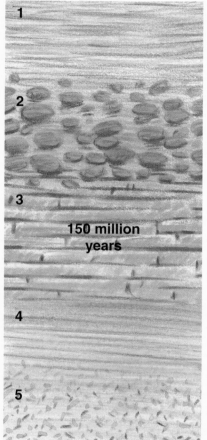

Look at the photo of the Grand Canyon in Arizona, USA. It was carved out by a river. Near the top of the canyon the rocks are 100 million years old. At the very bottom they are almost one billion years old.

If you dig down into the Earth and find a column of rock, you will find layers of different rocks, as shown on the left. Different rocks are made in different ways.

If the rocks have not been disturbed, the rocks at the bottom will be the oldest. The rocks then go up in order of age. The youngest rock is at the top.

d Where is the oldest rock in an undisturbed column of rock, at the top or at the bottom?

If we find a fossil of an animal that we know only lived between 100 and 110 million years ago, then we can tell that the rock that the fossil was found in is between 100 and 110 million years old. This sort of information helps us to find out what was happening on Earth at different times in the past.

e A rock contains a fossil of an animal that lived between 70 and 85 million years ago. What is the oldest age that the rock could be?

Questions

1. Copy and complete these sentences. Use words from the word wall to fill the gaps.

rocks	fossils	animals
plants	millions	hundreds

Geologists use _____ to find out about living things that existed _____ of years ago. Fossils are the remains of _____ and _____ that have been preserved in rocks.

2. Answer the following questions using the diagram above left.
  a Which layer of rock is the oldest?
  b Which layer of rock is the youngest?
  c Which layers are older than 150 million years old?

3. Make up a poem about being an Earth detective. Use these words:

fossils   rock   dig

Rock breaking

Rocks and minerals

There are many types of rock, each type made up from different elements and compounds called **minerals**. There are more than 2000 known minerals, but most rocks are made from just 12 of them.

a What is a mineral?

Rain and ice

Look at the photo. The bits of rock at the bottom of the slope used to be part of the mountain. They were broken off the side of the mountain and then worn away into smaller chunks. This is called **weathering**.

When rock is broken into smaller pieces, but not changed into different substances, we call this **physical weathering**. This can be caused by the effect of wind, water and changes in temperature. This is a physical change as no new substances are formed.

Water expands when it freezes. You may know that if the water in house pipes freezes, it will expand and burst the pipes. Most rocks have a lot of small cracks in them. Some rocks are **porous**, which means they have tiny holes like a sponge. Water can get into these cracks and holes.

When this water freezes, it expands and makes the cracks bigger. Later, the ice thaws and more water gets into the cracks and freezes again. This makes the cracks even bigger. In the end the rock breaks apart. This process is called **freeze-thaw**.

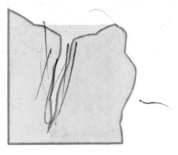

1. Water gets into cracks in the rock.

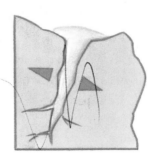

2. The water freezes and it expands.

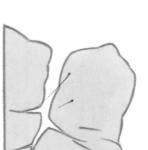

3. The force of the ice makes the crack bigger.

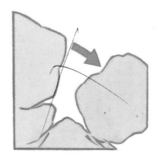

4. Eventually the crack gets so big that part of the rock breaks off.

b What happens to water as it freezes?

Hot and cold

In a desert it is very hot during the day, but it can get very cold at night. During the day, the hot rocks expand. During the cold nights, they contract. Rocks are mixtures of different minerals. Some minerals expand more than others. This creates big forces on the rock.

This happens every day and night, causing cracks to appear in the rock. The rock breaks apart into smaller rocks. These are finally weathered down to small grains of sand.

expansion   contraction   stresses in the rock cause it to crack

c What happens to rocks when they get hot?

d What happens to rocks when they get cold?

Wind

Rocks can also be worn away by the wind. Fine grains of sand can be blown against the rock and wear it away. On a beach you can often feel grains of sand being blown against your skin.

These strangely shaped rocks are called hoodoos. The hard rock on top has helped to protect the rock below it from being weathered. The rock around the outside has been worn away by the wind, leaving the hoodoo standing.

e How can rocks be worn away by the wind?

Questions

1. Copy and complete these sentences.

When rock is broken into smaller pieces, but not _____ into different _____, we call this _____ **weathering**. This can be caused by the effect of _____, water and changes in _____.

2. Explain three different ways in which a rock could be weathered.

3. Plan an experiment to prove that a rock could be weathered by being heated and cooled. What equipment would you need? What safety precautions would you need to take?

For your notes

Physical weathering happens when rocks are broken down into smaller pieces but not changed into different substances.

Physical weathering can be caused by water, wind and changes in temperature.

95

Disappearing rocks

7.3

Acid and rocks

Weathering is not only caused by wind and water. It can be caused by chemicals in the air and water around us. This is called **chemical weathering**. Chemical changes take place in the rock. Chemicals in the air and water react with minerals in the rock and form new substances. In the photo below, chemical weathering has changed the colour of the stone.

Air contains carbon dioxide. This dissolves in rainwater to make a solution that is slightly acidic. When this acid falls on some rocks, it starts to dissolve them.

The photo shows some rainwater being tested using a pH probe. The probe shows the pH of the water.

a Is the water acidic or alkaline?

b Why is the pH probe more precise than using universal indicator paper?

Many statues and buildings are made of a rock called **limestone**. Limestone is made of calcium carbonate. When acid falls on limestone, a chemical reaction happens. The limestone is completely changed by the acid. A new substance is formed which is soluble in water. Carbon dioxide is given off.

c Copy and complete this word equation for the reaction between an acid and a carbonate.

acid + carbonate → _____ + _____ + _____

Soil

When rock is chemically and physically weathered, it gradually turns into **soil**. The top layer of soil is called **topsoil**. This contains tiny grains of sand and clay and also decayed plant and animal matter called **humus**. Humus is rich in minerals that plants need for growth. Larger pieces of rock remain in the soil as stones.

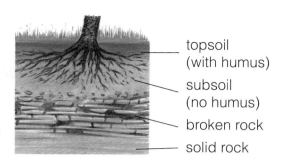

topsoil (with humus)

subsoil (no humus)

broken rock

solid rock

Acid rain

In the last 200 years, the rain has been becoming more acidic. There is more about acid rain on page 15. Acid rain causes rocks, statues and buildings to be weathered more quickly.

3. Acidic gases dissolve in rainwater in clouds.

4. Clouds are blown by the wind.

2. These gases rise into the air.

5. Acid rain then falls.

d What causes acid rain?

e Why is it becoming more of a problem?

1. Car exhausts and factories produce acidic gases.

Here are some ideas to reduce acid rain.

- Use cars less often.
- Use electric cars.
- Use more public transport.
- Put filters in factory chimneys to stop them giving off acidic gases.
- Use ways of making electricity that don't produce pollution.

Questions

1. Copy and complete these sentences. Use some words from the word wall to fill the gaps.

chemicals	sand	weathering	changes	substances	wind

Chemical _____ can be caused by _____ in the air and water around us.
Chemical _____ take place in the rocks and new _____ are made.

2. Write these statements in the correct order to describe how acid rain is produced.

- Raindrops fall as acid rain.
- Acidic gases rise into the air.
- Cars and factories produce acidic gases.
- Acidic gases dissolve in rain droplets in clouds.

3. Give two ways that soil is important for plants.

4. Write a letter to your local MP explaining about the problems of acid rain and telling him or her what could be done to reduce the problem.

For your notes

Chemical weathering is caused by reactions between acidic rainwater and minerals in the rock.

Soil forms when rocks are weathered.

Acid rain contains polluting gases dissolved in water.

97

Transporting rock

Where did it go?

When this house was built, it was a long way from the edge of the cliff. Over the years the cliff has gradually been weathered away and has collapsed into the sea. Finally the edge of the cliff was so close that the house was in danger of collapsing too.

The loose pieces of rock from the cliff are **transported** away by the movement of the waves and currents in the sea. They are worn away further. This is called **erosion**.

a Explain why the house is falling into the sea.

Transport and erosion can be caused by moving water, the wind or glaciers. Small pieces of rock are transported from one place to another more easily than large ones.

Wind

The wind can only blow small, light grains of sand. It cannot carry large pieces of rock because they are too heavy. If the wind is strong it may be able to carry slightly larger grains of sand, as in this desert sandstorm.

b Why do you think a strong wind can carry bigger grains of sand than a gentle breeze?

Glaciers carve out U-shaped valleys.

Glaciers

A **glacier** is a river of ice. Glaciers move very slowly, sometimes only one metre a month! As they move, they scrape the rock below them. The rock gets pushed along by the glacier. Glaciers can push rocks of all sizes, even very large boulders.

c What does the land look like after it has been eroded by a glacier?

Water

Rivers can carry large amounts of rock away from mountains and hills. Rivers move very fast near to their source in the mountain. Here the water can transport quite large pieces of rock. Rivers move more slowly when they get close to the sea. Here they can only carry small grains of rock.

d Which will be able to carry larger rock fragments, a mountain stream or a large river near the sea? Explain your answer.

Deposition

As a river slows down, it can no longer carry along large pieces of rock. They settle to the bottom of the river. This is called **deposition**. When the river is travelling very slowly, only very fine grains of rock can be carried along. The fine bits that settle out are called **sediment**.

An **estuary** is a river mouth where a slow-moving river flows into the sea. Layers of sediment build up here. Eventually there is enough sediment to form new land, and the river runs over it in lots of small streams. This is called a **delta**.

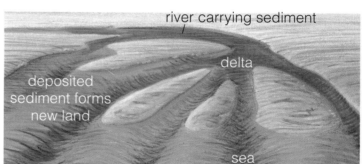

river carrying sediment

delta

deposited sediment forms new land

sea

e Why do you get a lot of sediment at the mouth of a river but not near its source?

Questions

1. Copy and complete the following sentences.

   Erosion happens when weathered rock is _____. Rock can be eroded by _____, _____ or _____. Fast-moving wind and water can carry _____ pieces than _____-moving wind or water. When the wind or water is no longer moving fast enough to carry the rock pieces, they are _____.

2. You are a lump of rock next to the river on the side of a mountain. You are hit by a large stone and washed into the river. Describe your journey to the sea.

For your notes

Erosion happens when rock is **transported** away from where it was weathered. Erosion wears away the rock pieces and makes them rounded.

Rock can be eroded by wind, water or **glaciers**.

Fast-moving wind and water can carry larger pieces of rock than slow-moving wind or water.

Deposition happens when pieces of rock that were transported settle again on to the Earth's surface.

Making rocks

The rock cycle

There are three main types of rock, and they change from one type to another over millions of years. This is called the **rock cycle** and it is shown in the diagram below.

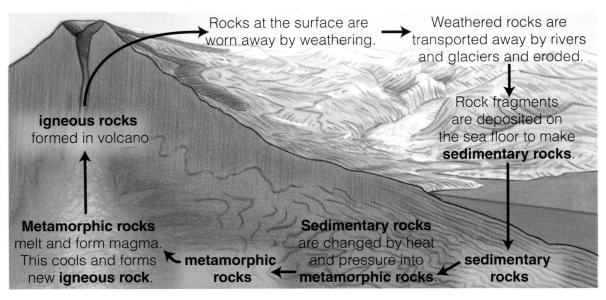

Rocks at the surface are worn away by weathering. → Weathered rocks are transported away by rivers and glaciers and eroded.

igneous rocks formed in volcano

Rock fragments are deposited on the sea floor to make **sedimentary rocks**.

Metamorphic rocks melt and form magma. This cools and forms new **igneous rock**. ← **metamorphic rocks** ← **Sedimentary rocks** are changed by heat and pressure into **metamorphic rocks**. ← **sedimentary rocks**

Igneous rocks

Igneous rocks are formed out of molten rock or **magma** from deep within the Earth. The magma is pushed up to the top layer or **crust** of the Earth. When the magma reaches the surface it is called **lava**. Sometimes the magma is forced out and **erupts** from a volcano, as shown in the photo below.

At the surface, the lava cools quickly and forms igneous rock with small crystals. **Basalt** is this sort of rock. Sometimes the magma never reaches the surface but cools slowly underground. This forms igneous rock with large crystals. **Granite** is this sort of rock.

ⓐ What is magma?

ⓑ What happens to the magma when it cools: **i** quickly? **ii** slowly?

Sedimentary rocks

Sedimentary rocks are formed from sediments. These are made up of small pieces called **grains** of rock and dead organisms. Sediments build up in layers over millions of years at the bottoms of lakes or seas. The photo below shows the layered structure of sedimentary rocks.

The pressure of the layers building up squeezes water out. The grains are left behind. These become stuck together under the pressure.

Sedimentary rocks such as **limestone**, **mudstone** and **sandstone** are formed in this way. Sedimentary rock is a bit like a sandwich: built from the bottom up in layers.

(c) What are sedimentary rocks made of?

(d) Why do you think sedimentary rocks often have fossils in them?

Metamorphic rock

Metamorphic rock is formed when existing rocks are changed by heat or high pressure. As the rocks become buried deeper in the Earth, the temperature and pressure become higher. This causes the minerals to change chemically without the rocks actually melting. New minerals form as crystals. **Slate** is an example of a metamorphic rock.

If the sedimentary sandwich was put into the oven, the heat would cause chemical changes in the bread and the fillings. The sandwich would look and behave very differently when it came out of the oven.

(e) Describe in what ways a baked sandwich might look and behave differently from an unbaked one.

Completing the cycle

If metamorphic rocks become buried very deep, eventually the temperature becomes so high that the rocks melt and turn to magma again.

Questions

1. Copy and complete the following sentences.

   The three rock types change from one to another over _____ of years. Igneous rocks are made from molten rock called _____. Small grains that become pressed together into layers become _____ rock over millions of years. Rocks can become buried, and under heat and pressure they can change into _____ rock.

2. Write the following parts of the rock cycle in the correct order:

   **deposition   weathering   rocks melt
   erosion   sedimentary rocks form
   burying and squeezing   volcanic eruption**

For your notes

The three main types of rock, **igneous**, **sedimentary** and **metamorphic**, are made in different ways.

They change from one type to another over millions of years.

These changes are summarised in the **rock cycle**.

Rock types

What are rocks?

Rocks are found everywhere. We walk on them and build with them. All rocks are made up of minerals. Different rocks are made up of different minerals or different mixtures of minerals.

a What are rocks made from?

How hard?

The hardness of a mineral can be measured by using the **Mohs scale**. This is a number scale from 1 to 10. A mineral that is very soft such as talc is 1 on the scale. A mineral that is very hard such as diamond is 10. A fingernail is 3 on the scale.

b You cannot scratch a diamond with your fingernail. Why not?

Rock types

We classify rocks into three main types, which are **igneous**, **sedimentary** and **metamorphic**.

Igneous rocks

These rocks are very hard and made of crystals. We say they are **crystalline**. In basalt these crystals are too small to see, but in granite the crystals are large. Igneous rocks are used for building and for road surfaces.

c Name an igneous rock that has small crystals.

Sedimentary rocks

Sedimentary rocks are made up of grains of other rocks or the remains of living things. Limestone is made from bits of calcium carbonate, which came from the shells of small sea animals. You can test rocks with hydrochloric acid to see if they contain calcium carbonate. The acid reacts with the calcium carbonate and fizzes to produce carbon dioxide.

Sandstone is made from grains of sand. Limestone is used for building roads and houses. It is also used to make toothpaste and make-up.

Diamond.

Talc.

Basalt.

Granite.

Limestone.

Sandstone.

Metamorphic rocks

Metamorphic rocks are hard and are made of small crystals often arranged in layers. Slate and **marble** are examples of metamorphic rocks. Slate comes from a sedimentary rock called **shale**. Marble comes from limestone.

Slate.

Marble.

Slate is used to make roofs. Marble is often used as a building material or for sculptures.

Properties of rocks

The properties of six different types of rock are summarised in the table below. These include grain or crystal size, hardness, colour and chemical reactions.

Rock	Properties
Basalt	A dark rock with very small crystals. There are no layers and it does not react with acid.
Granite	A hard rock with large crystals. There are no layers and it does not react with acid.
Shale	Usually a grey colour. It has very clear layers and often has fossils in it. Shale does not fizz with acid.
Slate	Usually grey, but sometimes it can be green or red. It can easily be split into layers. Fossils are not found in slate and it does not react with acid
Limestone	A pale, hard rock. It often contains fossils. Limestone fizzes with acid.
Marble	A hard rock that is normally white. It is made of tiny crystals and has no fossils or layers. It fizzes with acid.

d List the six rocks in the table, and say whether each is igneous, sedimentary or metamorphic.

Questions

1. For each rock type below, give one example and one way that we could use it. Which property makes it useful?
   a sedimentary
   b metamorphic
   c igneous

2. **a** Give one property that both granite and basalt have in common.
   b How can you tell the difference between granite and basalt?

3. **a** Name two rocks from these two pages that react with acid.
   b What does this reaction tell you about these rocks?

For your notes

Rocks can be classified according to their properties, such as grain or crystal size, hardness, colour and chemical reactions.

Igneous rocks are very hard and are made up of crystals.

Sedimentary rocks are made up of grains in layers, and often have fossils in them.

Metamorphic rocks are hard and are often made of crystals arranged in layers.

7.1

Name that rock

Why and what?

These words are all question words. Questions are very important in science:

Why? *What?* *How?* *Which?* *Where?*

● Scientists carry out investigations to find out the answers to questions. It is important to ask the right kinds of questions if you want to find out anything useful.

● Scientists use questions when they are classifying things and putting them into groups. A key is a set of questions that helps us to classify things.

Out in the field

Class 8T are on a geology field trip. They are looking at the rocks around them and testing them with acid. They are collecting small samples of different rocks to take back to the classroom. There they will find out about the properties of each rock, so they can look up in a reference book what sort of rock it is.

Before they go, Lisa, Grant and Hassan discuss the kinds of questions they will need to ask and answer about each rock sample. Read their suggestions.

We need to know: 'Is it made up of grains?' We can ask: 'Does the rock have any layers in it?'

We need to ask: 'What colour is the rock?' We could ask: 'What are the crystals like?'

How about asking: 'Does it react with acid?' 'What is the rock made up of?' 'Does the rock have crystals?'

Think about

▶ Classification

a In your group, consider each of the questions they suggest. Decide which questions would be the most useful when identifying rocks.

b Try to explain why each of the useful questions will be useful.

c See if you can come up with some more useful questions in your group.

Identifying the rocks

Look at these photos of the rocks Hassan's group brought back.

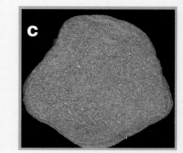

d Use the useful questions to help you to identify each of the three rocks.

Back at the classroom, Lisa's group found they hadn't kept careful enough notes about their samples. To make matters worse, Lisa had felt ill by the end of the field trip and had gone straight home. She took the group's three rock samples with her.

The rest of the group put together the notes they had. These are shown here.

e Look at the information Lisa's group brought back. Draw up a table with headings for the different properties rocks have. Look back at page 103 to remind you. Make three rows numbered 1 to 3 for the three rock samples.

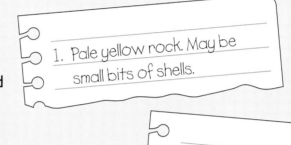

1. Pale yellow rock. May be small bits of shells.

f From the notes Lisa's group brought back, write in your table under the correct property what you already know about the three rock samples.

2. Contains pink, white and grey coloured bits in the rock. Doesn't react with acid.

g Look at the gaps in your table where you don't have any information. In your group, write down the questions you would need to answer in order to find out about the properties of the rock and identify it.

3. Contains large black flat crystals which are lined up. Some pale crystals. Very hard.

Questions

1. Write a key to classify the three main types of rock – sedimentary, igneous and metamorphic. Use your table and the questions you have written, and what you know about the properties of these three main types of rock.

2. Discuss what kinds of questions are best for classifying things. Explain your answer.

3. Why is it important to record observations from a field trip carefully?

No relief road!

Eco-warriors

Bailiffs swooped to evict eco-warriors from the protest camp on the route of the Northern Relief Road today.

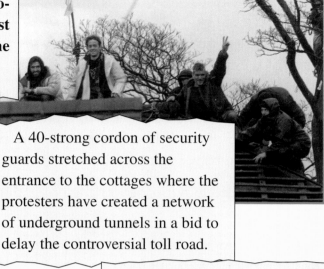

Police blocked off the entrance to the A38 at Bassetts Pole roundabout as the bailiffs approached the camp near Weeford.

A 40-strong cordon of security guards stretched across the entrance to the cottages where the protesters have created a network of underground tunnels in a bid to delay the controversial toll road.

'The role of the police at the site is to ensure the safety of the public.'

Why have a road?

The Northern Relief Road is a 27-mile long road which will take some of the traffic from the M6 motorway that goes through Birmingham. The M6 regularly has big traffic jams and accidents because it is so busy.

The relief road will destroy large areas of countryside. This will affect many of the plants and animals that live there. The place where a plant or an animal lives is called its **habitat**. The surroundings in a habitat are called the **environment**. A habitat provides all the things plants and animals need to carry out the life processes, and also gives them shelter. The road will remove lots of different habitats.

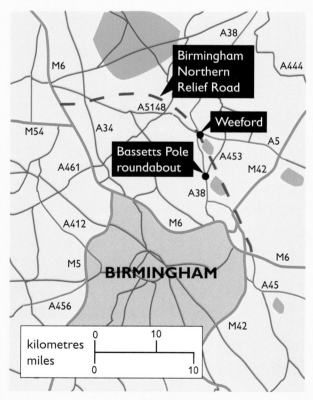

Different habitats

A habitat might be on land or in water. Examples of land habitats include fields, forests, soil and deserts. Water habitats include ponds, rivers or lakes and even salty water like the sea.

A habitat can be:
- hot or cold
- damp or dry
- light or dark.

a Make a list of all the different habitats that might be destroyed by the road.

Plants and animals have adaptations that help them to survive in their habitat, so we find different plants and animals in different habitats.

b I have a swollen stem and spiky leaves to save water. What am I? What is my habitat?

c I can fly, so I shelter from my predators high up in the trees. What am I?

Ecosystem

One area like a forest or pond, including all the living things in it and also its soil, air and climate, is called an **ecosystem**.

The ecosystem of a wood has lots of shade. The air is often cool and moist. Trees provide good nesting sites for birds and homes for climbing animals. There are lots of nuts and berries for them to eat in the autumn.

d This photo shows a very different ecosystem – a city. Describe what this ecosystem is like. Think about:
- air • temperature
- food for animals
- space for animals to live.

Decision time ...

Pete wants to help protect the ecosystems threatened by the road. He is thinking about joining the protest camp.

e Pete's friends ideas are shown here. Make a list of ideas for joining the camp. Make another list of ideas against joining the camp. Add more ideas of your own to each list.

f What do you think about the road? Would you do anything about it? Explain your reasons.

> The eco-warriors won't win – let's campaign to stop people using cars so much instead.

> These places are lovely to visit and it's sad to lose them.

> Why should we destroy other animals' homes?

> If they don't build the road the M6 will get worse.

Questions

1. Write out each word along with its explanation.

Words	Explanations
habitat	plants and animals having features that help them to survive
environment	place where a plant or animal lives
adaptation	surroundings in a habitat
ecosystem	area with living things together with the soil, air and climate

2. An oak tree is about to be cut down in the school grounds to extend the bike sheds. How would you feel about this? What would you do?

Putting plants into groups

Plants in their habitats

There are millions of types of plants. We call a group of plants of the same type a species.

Plants make up a large part of the environment. They provide food and shelter for animals. Scientists classify the millions of plant species into groups to make them easier to study. There are four main groups of land plants:

- flowering plants
- mosses
- ferns
- conifers.

Flowering plants

Grasses are flowering plants.

Silver birch trees are flowering plants.

The biggest group of plants is the **flowering plants**. These include grasses and many trees.

Flowering plants **reproduce** using **seeds**. The seeds are produced inside the **flowers**.

Some flowering plants attract insects to spread their pollen. They have large brightly coloured flowers. Others spread their pollen on the wind. They may have small dull flowers.

Different flowering plants have different shaped leaves. The leaves have a waterproof waxy layer called a **cuticle** on their top surfaces.

a What are flowers for?

Did you know?

Flowering plants can grow in dry places where many other plants would fail. This is because they have good systems for reproduction and transporting water.

Mosses

Mosses are small plants that look like a springy cushion. Mosses do not make seeds. They reproduce by making **spores**. They have very small, simple leaves, stems and small roots. Mosses do not have **veins** to carry water as other plants do. Mosses dry up easily because their leaves do not have a cuticle. This is why they have to live in wet places.

b Why would you be more likely to find mosses growing near a duck pond under an oak tree than in the middle of a field?

Ferns

Ferns do not make seeds. Like mosses, they reproduce by making **spores**, and they need moisture for this. Ferns have large, tough leaves called **fronds**. They also have strong stems and roots. Ferns grow well in damp, cool, shaded woodland habitats.

Conifers

Conifers are trees with a large trunk and roots. Conifers produce seeds inside **cones**. They have thin needle-like leaves with a cuticle to save water. Conifers can live in very cold, frozen climates.

Did you know?

The largest land habitat in the world is coniferous forest.

c Where are you most likely to find conifers? In:
i   a hot desert?
ii the slopes of a snow-covered mountain?
iii a wet peat bog?

d Copy and complete the flow chart showing how we classify plants.

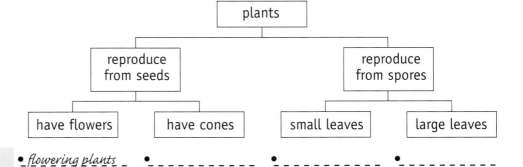

```
                        plants
              ┌───────────┴────────────┐
      reproduce                    reproduce
      from seeds                   from spores
     ┌────┴────┐                 ┌────┴────┐
have flowers  have cones    small leaves  large leaves
```

• *flowering plants*   •_____   •_____   •_____

Questions

1. Copy and complete the following sentences. Choose from the words below to fill the gaps.

   **conifers   dry   ferns   flowers   mosses
   seeds   spores   wet   flowering**

   The _____ plants are the only group of plants that have _____. Like the _____, they reproduce by making _____. The _____ dry out easily and so are found in _____ places.

2. Which type of forest would you expect to find in the Arctic?

3. Which plant groups can survive in most land habitats? Give a reason for your answer.

For your notes

Plants are classified into four groups by looking at their leaves and how they **reproduce**:

- **Flowering plants** reproduce from **seeds** and have various shapes of leaves.

- **Mosses** reproduce from **spores** and have very small leaves.

- **Ferns** reproduce from **spores** and have leaves called **fronds**.

- **Conifers** reproduce from **seeds** in **cones** and have thin, needle-like leaves.

109

Plants go for energy

Energetic forests

Like animals, plants need energy to carry out their life processes. Plants make their own food by photosynthesis, taking in light energy which is absorbed by chlorophyll. Plants need carbon dioxide and water for photosynthesis. They take in carbon dioxide through their leaves and water through their roots.

carbon dioxide + water → glucose + oxygen   light energy taken in

In the daytime, when it is light, plants take in carbon dioxide from the air and use light energy from the Sun for photosynthesis. Photosynthesis produces a sugar called **glucose**. It also makes oxygen as a waste product. Photosynthesis transfers light energy to chemical energy. At night, when it is dark, photosynthesis does not happen.

Respiration

Plants and animals break down their food to release the chemical energy from it. This process is called **respiration** and it happens in all plant cells just as it does in animal cells. Glucose and oxygen react, producing carbon dioxide and water, and releasing energy.

a Where in a plant does respiration take place?

b Write a word equation for respiration.

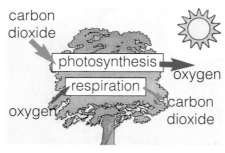

Photosynthesis is faster than respiration.

The whole picture

Respiration happens all the time, day and night. In the daytime, a plant gets its oxygen for respiration from photosynthesis.

During the day, photosynthesis is faster than respiration, so plants give out the oxygen they don't need into the air. At night photosynthesis stops, so plants take oxygen out of the air for respiration.

c Which gas do plants use for respiration?

d Which gas do plants make during the day and at night?

Root cells need oxygen from the air for respiration too. If the soil is waterlogged, all of the air spaces in the soil are filled with water. The roots cannot get enough oxygen and the plant will die.

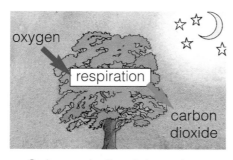

Only respiration takes place.

For my next experiment ...

Professor Chloe Dupont was trying to convince her students that both plants and animals respire. She set up a respiration chamber to show them that plants produce carbon dioxide by respiration. The respiration chamber apparatus is shown below.

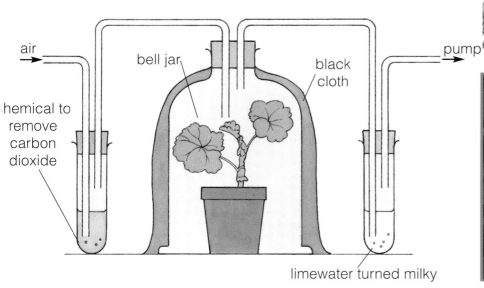

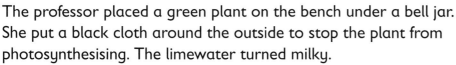

The professor placed a green plant on the bench under a bell jar. She put a black cloth around the outside to stop the plant from photosynthesising. The limewater turned milky.

e Why did photosynthesis stop?

f How do we know that the plant was respiring?

Did you know?

If you cut down the trees in a rainforest, you cut down the oxygen for us to breathe as well!

Questions

1. Copy the table and complete it using ticks and crosses to show which gases a plant uses and produces. The first row has been done for you.

2. Plants are often taken out of hospital wards at night. Can you think of a reason for this?

3. Which process only takes place during the day, photosynthesis or respiration? Explain your answer.

4. Chopping down rainforests gives us more land to graze cattle, so we can have cheaper burgers. What are the disadvantages of this?

	Day	Night
Uses carbon dioxide	✓	✗
Produces carbon dioxide		
Uses oxygen		
Produces oxygen		

For your notes

Plants release energy from food by **respiration**, in the same way as animals do.

Respiration takes place in every cell of a plant.

Growing and growing

Green fingers

Plants need **carbon**, **hydrogen** and **oxygen** for growth. They get these elements from the glucose they make by photosynthesis. The plant uses some of the glucose it makes for respiration. It converts the rest of the glucose to substances it needs for growth:

- cellulose for cell walls
- starch to store energy
- fats and oils
- sugars.

Learn about

► Plant growth
► Biomass

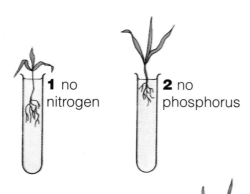

1 no nitrogen

2 no phosphorus

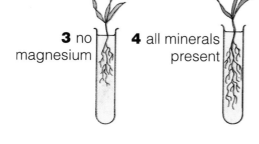

3 no magnesium

4 all minerals present

The plant also makes proteins and other substances. To make these substances from glucose, the plant needs other elements. It needs **nitrogen** for growth, and also **phosphorus** and **magnesium**. The plant takes them in through its roots from the soil. These elements are in **mineral salts** which are dissolved in water in the soil.

a Make a list of some of the elements a plant needs for growth.

Heather and Julie set up an experiment. They grew barley seedlings in water containing different mineral salts. Their results are shown on the left.

b Use their results to explain why plants need:
  i nitrogen   **ii** phosphorus   **iii** magnesium.

Feeling hungry

A caterpillar is a **herbivore**, which means it feeds on plants. This poem illustrates how much plant material a caterpillar needs to eat. The caterpillar kept on eating all week, but he was still hungry! A caterpillar needs a lot of energy because it rests for several weeks without eating while it turns into a butterfly.

He started to look for some food.

On Monday he ate through one apple. But he was still hungry.

c How do we know that a caterpillar is a herbivore?

d Why does a caterpillar need to eat so much food?

From "The Very Hungry Caterpillar" by Eric Carle.

Passing on biomass

All living things contain water. The total mass of a living thing, not including the water, is called its **biomass**. The biomass is made up of all the glucose made by photosynthesis, along with all the other substances in the plant such as starch, cellulose, fats and proteins. In a plant, photosynthesis produces the biomass of the plant. When a caterpillar eats a leaf, some of the plant biomass in the leaf becomes part of the caterpillar. Around 10% of the plant biomass eaten by a caterpillar becomes caterpillar biomass.

(e) Roughly how many grams of biomass might be transferred to a caterpillar that ate 100 g of cabbage leaves?

Where does the rest go?

Some of the food eaten by a caterpillar ends up as biomass in the caterpillar. The rest of the food eaten does not become caterpillar biomass. It is used to release energy in the caterpillar. The caterpillar uses this energy for the life processes such movement, reproduction and keeping warm. The rest of the food is excreted as waste.

Some of the food is used for respiration. This produces energy to move, reproduce, excrete and keep warm.

Some of the food is used for growth and becomes part of the caterpillar's body (biomass).

Some of the energy from respiration is wasted as heat energy lost to the surroundings.

Some of the food is not digested and passes out as waste.

Questions

1. Write out these sentences, putting the correct ending with each beginning.

Beginnings
The biomass of a living thing
Respiration produces energy from biomass

Some of the energy released from respiration
When a caterpillar eats, only some of the leaf biomass

Endings
and happens in all living things.
is all the material in it except the water.
becomes caterpillar biomass.
is used for the life processes.

2. A rabbit eats 1 kg of carrots. Use the caterpillar example to estimate its increase in biomass and explain why it does not become 1 kg heavier after its meal.

3. Write down the name of the element that a green plant needs to make chlorophyll.

For your notes

As well as **carbon**, **oxygen** and **hydrogen**, plants need **nitrogen** and other elements for growth.

The total mass of a living thing, not including the water, is called its **biomass**.

Some of the energy from the biomass eaten by an animal is used for growth so it is converted to animal biomass. The rest is used for the life processes or lost to the environment.

113

Woodland food chains

If you are walking through a wood in the spring or summer and look closely at the leaves, you might see a caterpillar feeding on a leaf. If you are patient, you might see the second link in the food chain – a bird swooping down to eat the caterpillar.

a What kind of animal do you think might eat the bird?

Learn about
► Food webs

A **food chain** shows the links between the organisms in an ecosystem. It shows which animals feed on other animals or on plants. The arrows show what eats what, and the direction of the energy transfer. Most food chains start with a plant. The plant makes its own food by photosynthesis using light energy from the Sun, carbon dioxide and water.

The green plants produce the food, so they are called **producers**. The animals consume (eat) the plants or other animals, so they are called **consumers**. Animals that eat plants, such as rabbits and field mice, are called **herbivores**. Larger animals such as foxes and owls, that eat other animals, are called **carnivores**. Energy is transferred through the food chain when one organism eats another.

Sun → grass → rabbit → fox

b Look at the food chain in the diagram. Which organism is:
i the producer? **ii** a herbivore? **iii** a carnivore?

Rabbits are not the only animals that eat grass.

c Can you think of another animal that eats grass?

Pyramids of numbers

A rabbit eats lots of grass plants. Several rabbits will feed just one fox. If you look at the number of producers, herbivores and carnivores in this food chain, you can build a pyramid.

d What happens to the number of consumers as you go up the pyramid?

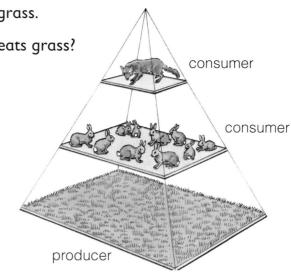

consumer

consumer

producer

114

Joan and Lydia used a **quadrat** to do their sampling. A quadrat is a wooden frame measuring one metre on all four sides. This means it has an area of one square metre.

Joan threw a quadrat over her shoulder without looking where it would land. Then she wrote down the number of rare daisy plants inside the quadrat.

She threw the quadrat and counted the daisy plants 10 times.

d Why did Joan throw the quadrat without looking where it would land?

Joan threw the quadrat down 10 times. Her sample was 10 times one square metre, so it was 10 square metres.

Throw number	Number of rare daisy plants
1	0
2	0
3	0
4	3
5	0
6	0
7	0
8	0
9	0
10	6

Joan's results

Joan and Lydia found 9 rare daisy plants in Joan's sample.

The whole sample has an area of 10 square metres. The field covers 4000 square metres in total. So the **ratio** of the area they sampled to the whole field is 1:400.

The ratio of the number of plants in the sample to the number of plants in the field is the same, 1:400. So to find the number of plants in the whole field, they multiplied the number in the sample by 400.

e How many rare daisy plants did Joan and Lydia think might be in the field?

f Will this be the exact number of plants in the field?

Questions

1. a How accurate do you think Joan and Lydia's experiments were?
  b How could they have made the experiments more reliable? Think about where the special daisy prefers to grow.

Flashes and bangs

The concert

There is going to be a concert to raise money for charity. Lots of local orchestras, choirs and bands are going to play at the concert. There will be fireworks. Amigo's father is in charge of the concert.

Rehearsals

Amigo goes with his father to see everything being set up. The concert is in a big field. There are two main stages: one for the orchestras and choirs and one for the bands. An orchestra is on stage, having a rehearsal. The musicians tune their instruments.

a What part of these instruments vibrates to make sound?

violin   drum   xylophone

b How does the music get from the violin to Amigo's ears?

Amigo goes over to the other stage. A band is rehearsing. They are trying to get the sound levels right. The band uses microphones, amplifiers and loudspeakers.

c Which device takes in sound energy and gives out electrical energy?

d Which device takes in electrical energy and gives out sound energy?

Amigo sits on the edge of the stage. He is so close that he can see the large cone of the loudspeaker moving in and out. Even with his fingers in his ears he can feel the music through the stage.

e Why does the cone of the loudspeaker move in and out?

f Why can Amigo 'feel' the music?

The performance

It was soon time for the concert to begin. Amigo was sitting with Gareth, a sound engineer from the local radio station. He listened as Gareth explained that it was difficult to broadcast a concert with so many different acts. Some of the acts were very loud and some were quieter. Some of the instruments were very high pitched and others made low-pitched sounds.

g Gareth measured the amplitude of the sounds. What does the amplitude of the sound tell Gareth?

h Gareth also measured the frequency of the sounds. What does the frequency of the sound tell Gareth?

Amigo loved the fireworks. One rocket was huge. It exploded high up in the air. Amigo saw the colours first, then he heard the sound the rocket had made when it exploded.

i Explain why Amigo saw the explosion before he heard it.

Amigo also saw a reflection of the firework in the water.

j How does Amigo see the firework in the water? Draw a diagram. Use arrows to show where the light is going.

Questions

1. Copy and complete this energy transfer diagram for a firework exploding.

2. Amigo saw the explosion before he heard it. Think of two other situations where you see something before you hear it.

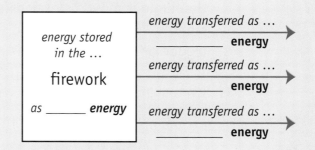

3. The fireworks were reflected in the lake. The lake was acting as a mirror.
   a Make a list of other things that can act as mirrors.
   b Why do these things act as mirrors?

4. Amigo heard two bangs. The first was the rocket exploding. The second was fainter. What was the fainter sound that Amigo heard later?

Travelling light

Sources and shadows

Sunlight comes from the Sun, or a candle, or a lamp. Light comes from a **source**. The source gives out light energy. The light energy travels away from the source in all directions.

a The Sun, a candle and a lamp are sources of light. Think of three other sources of light.

Light travels from the source in straight lines. If the light is blocked, a **shadow** is formed.

Look at the picture of the cinema. The source of light is the projector. The girl has walked between the source of light and the screen. The girl has blocked some of the light and there is a shadow on the screen.

b Imagine the girl was closer to the screen. Would the shadow be larger or smaller?

Learn about

▶ How light travels

▶ How we see light

Cameras

You can make a camera by making a hole in a piece of card with a pin. This is called a pinhole camera. You also need a screen to see the picture. Pinhole cameras work because light travels in straight lines.

c Look at the diagram showing how the pinhole camera works. Imagine that the flame is moved closer to the pinhole. Is the image on the screen bigger or smaller?

1. Some of the light from the top of the flame goes through the pinhole.

2. Some of the light from the bottom of the flame also goes through the pinhole.

pinhole in card

screen

3. A picture is made on the screen. This is called an **image**.

4. The image is upside down. We say the image is **inverted**.

5. The thing you look at using a camera or your eye is called an **object.**

122

More complicated cameras

Modern cameras are easier to use than pinhole cameras, and make much better pictures. The hole in a camera is called the **aperture**. The film inside the camera is protected by the **shutter**, which only opens when the picture is being taken. The camera contains a **lens**. The lens makes sure that the image is always sharp. We say that a sharp image is **in focus**.

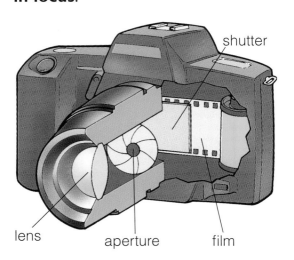

lens   aperture   film   shutter

Eyes

Some animals have very simple eyes, similar to a pinhole camera. Look at the diagram of a very simple animal eye. The small hole allows light into the eye. An upside down (**inverted**) image is made at the back of the eye. There are special cells at the back of the eye that are sensitive to light. They are shown in yellow.

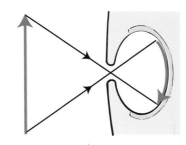

Our eyes are more complicated. Light enters the eye through the **pupil**. Each eye has a shutter, the eyelid, and a lens to make sure the image is always in focus.

Special cells in the back of the eye take in the light energy and give out electrical energy. Electrical signals go along nerves to the brain. The image on the back of the eye is inverted (upside down). Our brain turns the image the right way up.

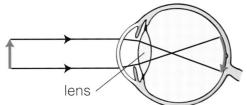

lens

d The hole for the light in a camera is called the aperture. What is the hole for the light in our eyes called?

Questions

1. Write out each word along with its definition.

Words	Definitions
image	something that gives out light energy
object	upside down
inverted	a picture
shadow	something being looked at using a camera or eyes
light source	darkness, where the light has been blocked

2. Copy and complete the following sentences to describe how an image is made:
   a in a pinhole camera
   b in an eye.
      i The light leaves …
      ii The light travels …
      iii The light enters the camera/eye through …
      iv The light is focused by …
      v The image forms …

For your notes

Light travels away from its source in all directions.

Light travels in straight lines.

We see because light enters our eyes.

Can you see it?

Geri is doing an experiment. She dresses in black clothes with black gloves and a black mask. She goes into a black room with no windows and shuts the door. It is dark.

Geri then turns on a light bulb. She can see the light bulb, but nothing else. The light travels from the light bulb to Geri's eyes.

Geri then takes a tennis ball out of her pocket. She can now see the ball. The light from the light bulb bounces off the ball and goes into Geri's eyes. When light bounces off a surface it is **reflected**. The light does not bounce off Geri's clothes or the walls because they are black. The light is soaked up when it hits a black surface. We say the light is **absorbed**.

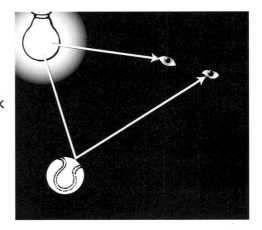

a In Geri's experiment:
  i What is the source of light?
  ii What surfaces absorb the light?
  iii What surfaces reflect the light?

A rule for reflection

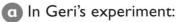

incoming ray   *reflected ray*

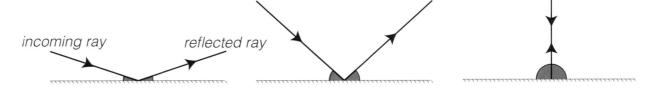

We can use a thin beam of light, a **ray**, to investigate reflection.

Look at the diagrams. A ray of light is hitting a flat surface in each diagram. There is a pattern in the way the ray is reflected. Look at the coloured angles. The angle between the ray and the surface is the same for the incoming ray and the reflected ray.

A

B

C

b Look at the diagram on the right. Which is the correct reflected ray, **A**, **B** or **C**?

Scattering

The paper of this book looks smooth, but it has many tiny bumps. The photo shows paper seen through a microscope. You can see the tiny bumps.

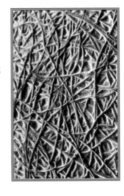

Look at the diagram. When light hits the paper, it is **scattered** in all directions. Most surfaces have tiny bumps, like the paper. Most surfaces scatter light.

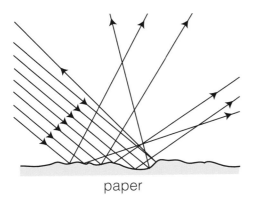

paper

c Why is the light scattered in all directions when it hits the paper?

Mirrors

A mirror is smooth. Look at the diagram. All the light rays are reflected in the same direction. The light is not scattered. You can see your image in a mirror because the light is not scattered.

d Why can you see your image in a mirror, but not in a piece of paper?

Using mirrors

Mirrors can be used to see around corners, or over a wall. Look at the diagram of a **periscope**. A periscope uses two mirrors so you can see what is happening above you.

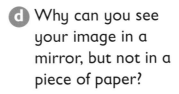

mirror

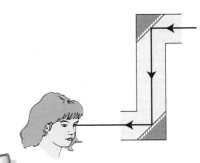

Questions

1. Copy and complete these sentences.
   a Black surfaces _____ light.
   b Light bounces off most surfaces. We say the light is _____. Very smooth surfaces reflect the light in the same direction, so we see an _____. Rough surfaces _____ the light.

2. Look at the diagram of a periscope.
   a What is the angle between the incoming ray and the mirror?
   b What is the angle between the reflected ray and the mirror?
   c Explain how you can use a periscope to look over a wall.

3. A puddle can act as a mirror. Use a diagram to explain this.

For your notes

When light hits a surface, it is **absorbed** or **reflected**.

The angle between the ray and the surface is the same for the incoming ray and the reflected ray.

Most surfaces **scatter** light.

Mirrors do not scatter the light because they are smooth.

125

Bending light

Transparent materials

Light goes through some materials, like glass and water. Glass and water are **transparent**, or see-through. Some materials let no light through, like wood and brick. Wood and brick are **opaque**. **Translucent** materials only let some of the light through. Thin paper is translucent.

A trick of the light

You sometimes see odd things when light goes through a transparent material like water or glass.

Light bends when it goes from air to water, or from glass to air. We call this bending **refraction**. The bending makes the pencil look bent, and the words look bigger.

a Light bends when it goes from air to water. What is the scientific word for this bending?

Learn about

▶ Refraction

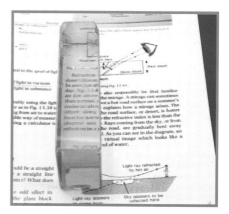

Air to glass

Light refracts (bends) when it goes from air to glass. The path of the light bends inwards.

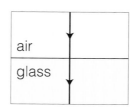
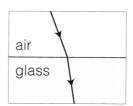
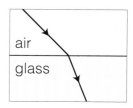

Look at the left-hand diagram. If the light enters glass straight (at 90°), the light does not bend. Look at the other two diagrams. When the ray of light hits the glass at an angle, it bends.

b Does the light bend (refract) when it hits the glass straight on?

Glass to air

The light also bends when it goes from glass to air. The path of the light bends outwards.

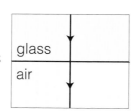
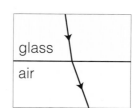
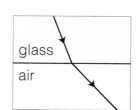

Again, if the ray hits straight on (at 90°), it does not bend.

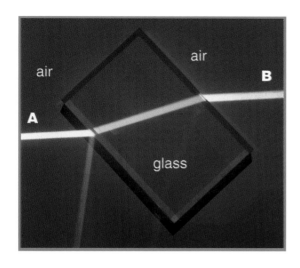

The glass block

When light goes through a glass block it goes from air to glass, then from glass to air. The light refracts when it goes from air to glass, then refracts again as it goes from glass to air.

Look at the photo. When the light goes from air to glass it bends inwards. When the light goes from glass to air it bends outwards. The light comes from **A**. It travels through the block and ends up at **B**.

Water to air

Refraction also happens when light travels from water to air. Look at the diagram on the right. Light from the coin is refracted when it goes from the water to the air.

Your brain thinks that light travels in straight lines. You see the coin higher up, where the light seems to come from.

c What happens when the light goes from the water to the air?

d The water above the coin seems shallower than it is. Why does your brain think that the water is shallower?

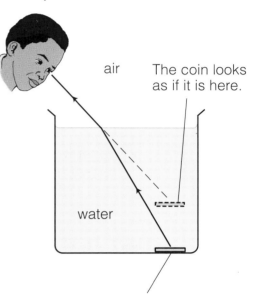

The coin looks as if it is here.

The coin is really here.

Questions

1. Copy and complete these sentences.

Light goes through _____ materials like water, air and glass. When the light enters a new transparent material at an _____, it bends. This bending is called _____.

2. Which is the correct ray in each diagram, **A**, **B** or **C**?

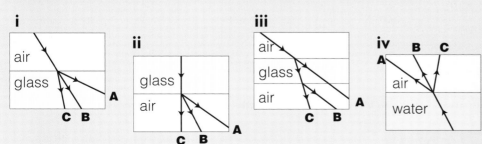

For your notes

When light goes from one **transparent** material to another, it may **refract** (bend).

The light must enter the new material at an angle for refraction to happen.

127

Coloured light

Splitting white light

A prism splits sunlight into many colours. We call the colours a **spectrum**. The splitting up is called **dispersion**. White light enters the prism and is separated into the colours of the spectrum. The colours are always in the same order: red, orange, yellow, green, blue, indigo and violet.

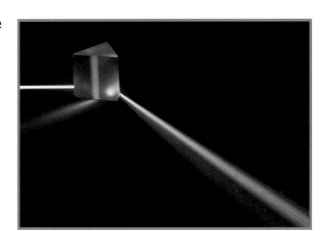

a What do we call:
  i the 'rainbow' of colours made using a prism?
  ii the splitting up of light?

Learn about

→ White light
→ Coloured light

Droplets of water can act as tiny prisms. The different colours bend by different amounts as they go through the drops. The colours are spread out, making a rainbow.

Did you know?

Many children in Britain learn the colours of the spectrum using this mnemonic:

Richard **of Y**ork **g**ave **b**attle **in v**ain.

Coloured filters

Look at the diagram of a stained glass window. Only red light comes through the red glass in the window. The red glass absorbs the other colours.

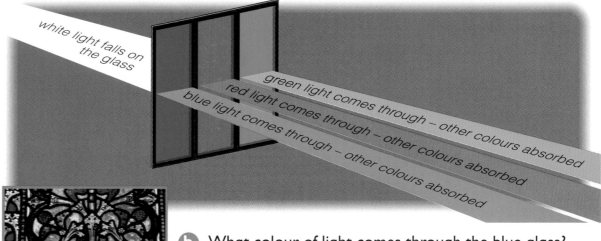

white light falls on the glass

green light comes through – other colours absorbed

red light comes through – other colours absorbed

blue light comes through – other colours absorbed

b What colour of light comes through the blue glass?

c Only green light comes through the green glass. What happens to the other colours in the light?

Seeing by reflection

A red surface reflects red light. The red light enters our eyes and we see red. If we shine white light onto a red surface, the red light is reflected and the other colours are absorbed.

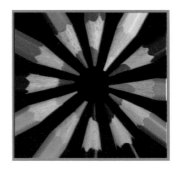

d What colour of light is reflected by a blue surface?

e What happens to red light when it hits a blue surface?

Photographers develop their film in a darkroom. The use a special red light to see. The red light does not affect the film.

Things look odd inside a darkroom when the red light is on. The photographer in the picture is wearing a white shirt, but it looks red. This is because there is only red light in the room. The white shirt reflects all colours of light, so it reflects the red light.

f What is the only colour of light in the darkroom?

g What colour of light is being reflected from the shirt?

The photographer is wearing green trousers, but they look black. This is because there is no green light for the trousers to reflect.

h Why do the photographer's trousers look black?

i What happens to the red light when it hits the photographer's trousers?

Questions

1. Conor is investigating light using coloured filters. He does the experiments shown in the diagram. What colours of light (if any) will he see at **A**, **B**, **C** and **D**?

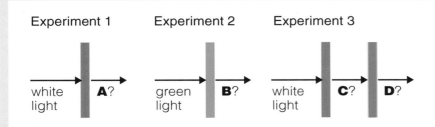

Experiment 1	Experiment 2	Experiment 3
white light → **A?**	green light → **B?**	white light → **C?** **D?**

For your notes

White light can be split into different colours. This is called **dispersion**.

A red, green or blue filter only allows one colour of light through and absorbs the others.

A coloured object reflects the colour we see and absorbs the other colours.

2. Eileen goes to a club. The club is having a 70s night with a disco. The lights flash green, blue and red. Eileen is wearing a white shirt, a red skirt and black boots.
   a The red light is on. What colour will Eileen's:
      i shirt be?   **ii** skirt be?   **iii** boots be?
   b The blue light is on. What colour will Eileen's:
      i shirt be?   **ii** skirt be?   **iii** boots be?

9.6

Colour combinations

Combinations

Joe's form has been collecting copper coins for a charity. Joe is counting the money and putting it into bags. There are three possible **combinations**: only 1p coins in a bag, only 2p coins in a bag or a bag of mixed 1p and 2p coins. The coins can be combined in three different ways, to make three different combinations. You can read more about combinations in the blue box on the opposite page.

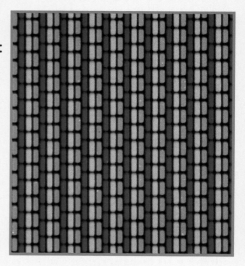

Primary colours of light

The photo shows a television screen close up. The screen is made up of red, green and blue dots.

Red, green and blue are the three **primary colours** of light. All colours of light can be made from combining these colours.

a How many different combinations can you make out of red, green and blue?

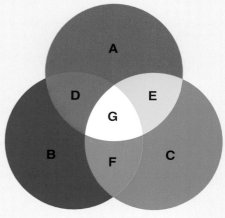

Secondary colours

Secondary colours of light are made by mixing red, green and blue light. Look at the colour chart. It shows what happens when you combine red, green and blue light. For example, colour **E** is made by combining **A** with **C**.

b Copy this table and use the colour chart to fill in the gaps.

Position	Colour	Which of red, green and blue?
A	Red	
B	Blue	
C	Green	
D	**Magenta**	
E	**Yellow**	
F	**Cyan**	
G	White	

Lighting the show

Zahir wanted to help with lighting for the school play. Miss Lawrence set him a test about colour.

c Do the 'Lighting test'. It is in the green box on the opposite page.

d Mark your answers (see the bottom of the next page).

Zahir could not do questions 6 and 7.

e Write down what you would say to explain questions 6 and 7 to him. Draw any diagrams that you would use.

An example of combinations

Jane has bought some decorations in a sale. She has stars, snowflakes and angels. How many different combinations can she make?

Jane can have each type of decoration on its own:

- stars
- snowflakes
- angels.

Jane can have 2 types of decoration together:

- stars and snowflakes
- stars and angels
- snowflakes and angels.

Jane can have 3 types of decoration together:

- stars, snowflakes and angels.

So there are 7 different types of combination.

Lighting test

Imagine you only have 3 spotlights, a red, a green and a blue. What combinations of red, green and blue do you use to make the following colours?

1. Yellow.

2. Cyan.

3. Magenta.

4. White.

You can change the colour of a spotlight by putting in different filters. What combination of <u>primary</u> colours gets through each filter? (Remember only red, green and blue are primary colours.)

5. Red filter.

6. Yellow filter.

7. Cyan filter.

Questions

1. Bernie is putting up fairy lights to celebrate the New Year. He has 4 different types of bulb that he can use:

   - red flashing
   - red
   - green flashing
   - green.

   What different combinations of bulbs could Bernie put in his string of fairy lights? List them all.

Answers to Lighting test

1. green and red   2. green and blue   3. red and blue   4. red, green and blue   5. red   6. red and green   7. blue and green

Sound is like light

Light and sound carry energy

Light and sound both come from a source. Light sources, like the Sun, give out light energy. Sound sources, like a whistle, give out sound energy.

Light can transfer energy. When light falls on a **solar cell**, the solar cell gives out electrical energy. The photo shows solar cells giving out energy.

energy transferred as … **light energy** → *solar cell* *energy transferred as …* **electrical energy**

Sound can transfer energy. When sound reaches a microphone, the microphone gives out electrical energy.

energy transferred as … **sound energy** → *microphone* *energy transferred as …* **electrical energy**

(a) Name three sources of light energy.

(b) Name three sources of sound energy.

Sound is reflected or absorbed

Some surfaces reflect light. A white surface reflects all colours of light. Other surfaces absorb light. Black surfaces absorb all colours of light.

Sound is also reflected from some surfaces. Reflected sound is called an **echo**. Other surfaces absorb sound. Sounds seem muffled when the ground is covered in snow. This is because there are very few echoes.

Recording studios are lined with sound-absorbing materials to prevent echoes. The echoes would ruin the recording.

(c) Why is it a good idea to prevent echoes in a recording studio?

Different materials, different speeds

Sound travels at different speeds in different materials, as this table shows.

Light also travels at different speeds in different materials. Light travels at 300 million m/s in air, 92 million m/s in glass and 225 million m/s in water.

Material	Speed of sound in m/s
Air (at 0 °C)	330
Water	1500
Wood (oak)	3850
Iron	5000

Refraction

Sound can refract (bend) when it goes from cooler air to warmer air. This can happen on a summer night. It is similar to light refracting when it goes from one transparent material to another. Look at the diagram on the right. The light bends every time it goes into a different type of glass.

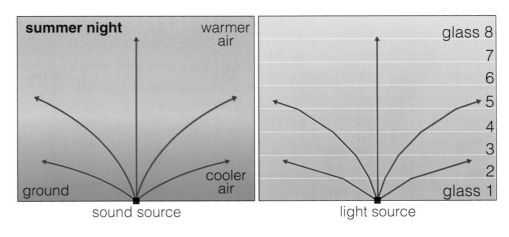

Frequency

A vibrating object makes a sound. The pitch of the sound depends on the frequency of the vibration (how often it vibrates in 1 second). Middle C has a lower frequency than the D note above it. The next C up has double the frequency of middle C. We talk about the frequency of light in a similar way. Different colours of light have different frequencies.

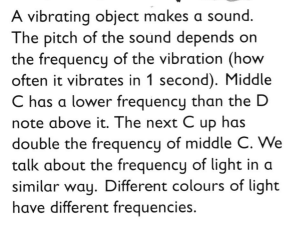

Did you know?

Isaac Newton, the famous scientist, decided that there were 7 colours in the spectrum because there were 7 notes in a scale of music.

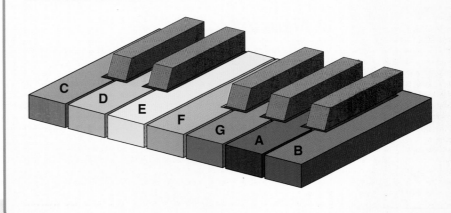

Questions

1. Sound and light both carry _____. Light or sound is _____ or _____ when it hits a surface. Reflected sound is called an _____. Both light and sound travel at different _____ in different materials. Sound can _____ when it goes from cooler air to warmer air. Light can also _____ when it goes from one type of glass to another type of glass. The _____ of sound and the _____ of light depend on the frequency.

2. Maria looks at the table opposite showing the speed of sound in different materials. She concludes that sound travels fastest in solids, slower in liquids and slowest in gases.

   What extra experiments should Maria do to test her conclusion?

For your notes

Sound and light carry energy.

Sound and light can be absorbed or reflected.

Sound and light travel at different speeds in different materials.

Sound and light can be refracted.

Sound and light can vary in frequency.

Sound is different from light

Speed

Light travels very, very fast. Light travels through air at 300 million m/s. Sound travels much slower. The speed of sound in air is about 330 m/s. In the time it takes for light to travel the length of a football pitch, sound would travel 0.1 mm.

Storms make both light, as lightning, and sound, as thunder. If a storm is 10 km away, the light from the lightning would reach you in 0.000 03 s, while the sound from the thunderclap would take 30 s to reach you. The longer the gap between the lightning and the thunder, the further away the storm.

(a) Which travels faster, sound or light?

Measuring the speed of sound

Janet and Luisa are measuring the speed of sound. Janet goes to the other end of the playing field. She measures the distance as she walks. The distance between Janet and Luisa is 300 m.

Luisa has a large wooden clapper. Janet starts her stopwatch when she sees Luisa close the clapper, and stops her stopwatch when the sound reaches her. Janet measures 0.95 s.

Janet and Luisa then work out the speed of sound. They put their values in this equation:

$$\text{speed} = \frac{\text{distance}}{\text{time}}$$

(b) Work out the speed of sound according to Janet and Luisa's first experiment.

Janet and Luisa then do five other experiments. Their measurements are shown in the table.

Experiment	1	2	3	4	5	6
Time in s	0.95	0.98	1.04	0.92	**0.98**	0.96

(c) Why are the measurements different?

Janet and Luisa use their values to work out an average time. They use this equation:

$$\text{average time} = \frac{\text{all the time values added up}}{\text{the number of values}}$$

d Work out an average time for the sound to travel 300 m.

e Work out an average speed for sound from Janet and Luisa's experiment.

Measuring the speed of light

It is very difficult to measure the speed of light, because light travels so fast. Albert Michelson was a scientist who measured the speed of light. He put a light source on the top of one mountain and a mirror on the top of another mountain. He measured the time light took to travel from the top of the first mountain to the top of the other mountain and back again. The mountains were 36 km apart and the light took just over 0.0002 s to make the journey there and back!

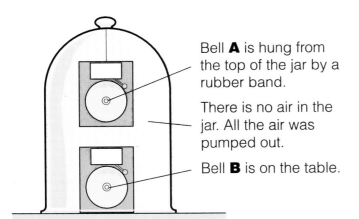

Bell **A** is hung from the top of the jar by a rubber band.

There is no air in the jar. All the air was pumped out.

Bell **B** is on the table.

Passing through

Light travels through any transparent material, or through empty space. Sound travels through solids, liquids and gases, but it cannot travel through empty space. Sound needs a material to travel through, but light does not.

f Look at the diagram of the two bells in a jar.
    i Would you hear bell **A**? Why?
    ii Would you hear bell **B**? Why?

Questions

1. Why do you see lightning before you hear thunder when a storm is far away?

2. Why does light travel through outer space but sound does not?

3. The speed of sound in water is 1500 m/s. Two whales are 3000 m apart. How long does it take sound to travel from one whale to the other?

For your notes

Light travels much faster than sound.

Sound needs a material to travel through. Light does not.

absorption   The process by which digested food passes through the lining of the small intestine into the blood.
   When light or sound is soaked up by a surface, it is absorbed.

acid   A solution that has a pH lower than 7.

acid rain   Rain polluted by acidic gases such as sulfur dioxide dissolved in it. Acid rain is more acidic than rainwater that is not polluted.

air pressure   The gas pressure caused when air particles all around us hit us and other surfaces.

algae   Organisms that make their food using sunlight. Some algae are single-celled.

alkali   A base that dissolves in water, forming a solution with a pH greater than 7.

alternative   Alternative energy resources are energy resources that are not fossil fuels.

anaemia   A disease caused by not eating enough iron in the diet, in which the person is pale and feels very tired.

anorexia nervosa   An eating disorder which causes a person to eat too little.

antagonistic pair   Two muscles that work against each other to move a bone at a joint. The muscles pull the bone in opposite directions.

anus   The opening through which undigested food passes out of the body.

aperture   A small opening.

artery   A blood vessel in which blood flows away from the heart.

arthritis   A disease of the joints, in which the joints become very swollen and painful.

artificial satellites   Satellites that are made by people.

asteroids   Rocky objects in space. In our Solar System most of the asteroids are found in the asteroid belt.

astronomy   The study of planets, stars and other objects in space.

axis   An imaginary line through the Earth that runs from the North Pole to the South Pole.

balanced diet   A diet that has the right amounts of all the nutrients.

ball and socket joint   A type of joint that allows a bone to move around in all directions, as in the shoulder or hip.

basalt   An igneous rock with small crystals.

base   A substance that reacts with an acid and neutralises it.

battery   An object that changes chemical energy into electrical energy.

biological washing powder   Washing powder that contains enzymes to break down stains.

biomass   The total mass of a living thing, not including the water.
   Biomass can be used as an energy source.

blood vessels   Tubes in which blood flows all around the body.

boiling point   The temperature at which a liquid changes into a gas.

calcium A metallic element. The mineral calcium is found in milk and cheese, and it keeps your teeth and bones healthy. The mineral calcium is actually calcium compounds.

calcium carbonate A basic compound present in some rocks such as limestone, chalk and marble.

calcium chloride The salt made when hydrochloric acid is neutralised with calcium carbonate.

canines Teeth for piercing and tearing meat.

capillary A very small blood vessel.

carbohydrates Nutrients found in foods such as bread, which give you energy.

carbon A non-metallic element present in fuels and in living things.

carnivore An animal that feeds on other animals.

cartilage A very smooth substance found on the ends of bones, which allows them to move over each other easily.

catalytic converter A device fitted to a car's exhaust that removes some polluting gases, such as carbon monoxide and nitrogen oxides, by chemical reactions.

chemical weathering The breaking up of rocks by chemicals in the environment. The substances in the rocks are changed into new substances.

chemicals Everything is made from different chemicals or substances. Chemicals can be either elements or compounds.

chloride A salt that is made by neutralisation of hydrochloric acid.

cilia Tiny hairs on the outside of some types of cell.

circulatory system An organ system that transports substances around the body.

coal Material from plants that lived millions of years ago, used as a fuel.

combination One way in which objects are put together.

comet A small object in the Solar System made of ice, dust and gas, that travels around the Sun.

compensation Making up for a change by balancing things out.

concentrated A solution that contains a lot of dissolved solute is concentrated.

concentration The amount of solute dissolved in a particular volume of a solution.

cones Structures that contain the seeds in conifers.

conifers Plants that reproduce from seeds in cones and have thin, needle-like leaves.

conserved When the same amount is there at the end as there was at the beginning. When a solid is dissolved in a liquid, the mass of solution equals the mass of solid plus the mass of liquid. The mass is conserved.

consumer An animal, that eats (consumes) plants or other animals.

contraction A material getting smaller as it cools down. When a muscle gets shorter, we say it is contracting.

corrosion Eating away of the surface of a solid by a chemical reaction.

corrosive Substances that may destroy living tissues on contact are corrosive.

crust The outer layer of the Earth.

crystalline A substance that contains crystals is crystalline.

cuticle A waterproof layer on the surface of some leaves.

cyan A colour of light produced by mixing blue and green light.

decomposer An organism that feeds on dead bodies of plants and animals.

delta New land formed by deposition at the mouth of a river.

deposition Small pieces of rock settling at the bottom of a river or the sea.

diffusion Gas or liquid particles spreading out as their particles move and mix.

digestion Process by which food is broken down into smaller molecules.

digestive system The organ system that breaks down your food into smaller molecules and absorbs them.

dilute A solution that does not contain much dissolved solute is dilute.

dioxins Waste products of industrial processes, that are toxic.

dispersion The splitting of white light into colours.

donate To give something, such as a healthy organ for transplant.

echo A reflected sound.

ecosystem An area such as a forest or a pond, including all the living things in it and also its soil, air and climate.

egestion Passing undigested food out of the body.

environment The surroundings in a habitat.

enzymes Substances that speed up the breakdown of food in digestion.

epithelial cells Special cells that make up the linings of your nose and throat. They make mucus to trap dust and germs.

erosion Loose pieces of rock are broken down while being transported.

eruption A volcano erupts when magma is forced out of it.

estimate An informed guess, usually applied to numbers.

estuary Where a river meets the sea.

evaluate To judge how good a model or experiment is, finding its good points and bad points.

expansion A material getting bigger as it heats up.

faeces The undigested food that is egested from the body.

fats Nutrients found in foods such as butter, that give you energy and insulate your body.

ferns Plants that reproduce from spores and have leaves called fronds.

fibre Bulky material found in cereals, fruits and vegetables which helps to keep food moving through your gut.

flower An organ system in flowering plants that produces seeds.

flowering plants Plants that reproduce from seeds made in flowers and have various shapes of leaf.

focused (in focus) When an image is sharp rather than fuzzy, it is focused or in focus.

food chain A diagram that shows how the organisms in an ecosystem feed on each other.

food web Lots of food chains link together to form a food web, that shows the feeding relationships in an ecosystem.

formula The ratio of different types of atoms in a compound.

fossil The remains of an animal or plant that have been buried deep underground for millions of years and preserved.

fossil fuels Materials from animals and plants that lived many millions of years ago, used as a fuel.

freeze-thaw Water inside a crack freezes and expands, exerting a force on the rock. The ice then thaws. This process is repeated many times until the rock eventually breaks apart.

fronds The large tough leaves of ferns.

function The job that something does.

galaxy A collection of millions of stars held together by gravitational pull.

gas pressure A pressure caused by gas particles hitting the sides of their container.

generator A device that takes in moving (kinetic) energy and gives out electrical energy.

geocentric model A model of the universe with Earth at the centre of the universe, and everything including the Sun moving around it.

geological time Long periods of time, during which processes happen over millions of years.

geologist A scientist who studies the Earth and rocks.

geostationary satellite A satellite that orbits the Earth at the same speed as the Earth is spinning on its axis, so it stays above the same part of the Earth's surface.

geothermal Heating by hot rocks under the ground.

glacier A slow-moving river of ice which can erode rocks by scraping across the top of them.

global warming An increase in the average temperature of the Earth.

glucose A small molecule formed by breaking down carbohydrates, or made by plants in photosynthesis.

grain A tiny piece of a material, such as sand.

granite A type of igneous rock with big crystals.

gravitational force The pulling force between one object and another. Gravitational force keeps objects in orbit around other objects.

gullet The part of the gut that links the mouth and stomach, also called the oesophagus.

gut The long tube in your body down which food passes between the mouth and the anus, and where digestion and absorption take place.

habitat A place where an organism lives, that provides all the things the organism needs to carry out the life processes.

haemoglobin   A chemical in red blood cells that carries oxygen around the body.

harmful   Harmful substances may have a health risk similar to but less serious than toxic substances.

heliocentric model   A model of the Solar System with the Sun at the centre of the Solar System and the planets moving around the Sun in circular orbits.

herbivore   An animal that feeds on plants.

hinge joint   A type of joint that allows a bone to move backwards and forwards.

humus   Dead animal and plant material found in soil. It provides plants with nutrients.

hydroelectric   Using the kinetic (movement) energy of falling water by changing it into electrical energy.

hydrogen   A non-metallic element that is an explosive gas.

igneous rock   Rock that is formed from molten lava or magma which has cooled and solidified.

image   An object seen indirectly on a screen or using a mirror or lens.

incisors   Teeth at the front of the mouth for tearing food.

indicator   A coloured substance that shows whether the solution being tested is acidic, alkaline or neutral.

inverted   Upside down.

iron   A metallic element. The mineral iron is found in liver and eggs, and it is used in your body to make blood.

irritant   Substances that can cause reddening or blistering in contact with the skin are irritant.

joint   A place in the skeleton where bones can move.

kinetic energy   Movement energy – the energy an object has because it is moving.

large intestine   The part of the gut where waste food is stored and water is absorbed.

lava   Molten rock from deep below the surface of the Earth which reaches the surface through cracks or volcanoes.

leaf   A plant organ that is important for photosynthesis.

leap year   A year that has 366 days, that occurs every four years.

lens   A piece of curved, transparent material used to bend light.

ligament   Strong tissue that holds bones together at a joint.

lime   A basic substance containing calcium oxide or other calcium compounds.

limestone   A type of sedimentary rock formed from the shells of sea creatures, which contains calcium carbonate.

line of best fit   A line drawn on a graph that shows the overall trend or pattern.

litmus   An indicator made from lichens.

luminous   Objects that give out light are luminous.

lunar eclipse   An eclipse that occurs when the shadow of the Earth moves across the Moon.

magenta   A colour of light produced by mixing red and blue light.

magma   Molten rock found deep below the surface of the Earth.

magnesium   A metallic element. Magnesium compounds are needed by plants. These compounds are sometimes called minerals or nutrients.

marble   A type of metamorphic rock that is produced when limestone is heated under high pressure.

melting point   The temperature at which a solid changes into a liquid.

metamorphic rock   Rock formed when sedimentary or igneous rocks are changed by intense heat and/or pressure.

meteor   A very small piece of debris from a comet.

meteorite   A solid mass of rock or metal from space that lands on Earth.

methane   A hydrocarbon with the formula CH_4.

mineral salts   Salts dissolved in water in the soil that provide the elements plants need for growth.

minerals   All rocks are made up of substances called minerals. Different rocks are made up of different minerals or different mixtures of minerals.
  Compounds of calcium and iron that are needed in the diet in small amounts to keep your body healthy are also called minerals.

mitochondria   Small structures inside cells where respiration takes place.

Mohs scale   A scale used for measuring the hardness of a mineral.

molars   Teeth at the back of the mouth for grinding.

molecule   A group of two or more atoms joined together.

mosses   Small plants that look like a springy cushion. They reproduce from spores and have very small leaves.

mudstone   A dark grey sedimentary rock.

muscle   Tissue that can contract. A muscle is an organ made up of muscle tissue along with other tissues such as capillaries.

natural gas   A gas formed from animals and plants that lived many millions of years ago, used as a fuel. It is mostly methane.

nervous system   An organ system that sends messages around the body.

neutral   A substance that is neither acidic nor alkaline, with a pH of 7, is neutral.

neutralisation   The chemical reaction that takes place when an acid reacts with a base.

nitrogen   A non-metallic element that is a gas present in the air.

non-luminous   An object that does not give out light is non-luminous.

non-renewable   A fuel (or other energy resource) that is not replaced as we use it is non-renewable.

northern hemisphere   The top half of the Earth.

nuclear   A process or device that involves radioactive materials is described as nuclear.

nutrients   Useful substances present in foods.

obese   People who are very overweight for their height are obese.

object   Something you look at using a mirror or lens to form an image.

oesophagus   The part of the gut that links the mouth and stomach, also called the gullet.

oil   A liquid formed from animals and plants that lived many millions of years ago, used as a fuel.

opaque   A material that does not allow light to pass through is opaque.

orbit   The path a satellite takes around the object it is travelling round.

organ   A group of different tissues that work together.

organ system   A group of organs that work together.

organ transplant   A damaged or diseased organ is removed and replaced with a healthy one from an organ donor.

organic food   Food that has been produced without using manufactured chemicals.

oxygen   A non-metallic element that is a gas. Oxygen is used in burning and in respiration.

partial eclipse   An eclipse viewed from a place where the shadow is not complete.

particle theory   A model that uses particles to explain why solids, liquids and gases behave the way they do.

periscope   A device used to see around corners.

peristalsis   Movements of the gut wall to push the food along.

petal   A plant organ that attracts insects to a flower.

pH scale   A number scale used to measure the strength of acidity and alkalinity.

phases of the Moon   The different shapes of the Moon seen as the Moon orbits the Earth.

phosphorus   A non-metallic element. Phosphorus compounds (mineral salts) are needed by plants for growth.

physical weathering   Breaking down rocks into smaller pieces, without changing them into new substances. Physical weathering can be caused by water, wind and changes in temperature.

pivot joint   A type of joint that allows bones to move in a circular motion.

polar orbit   An orbit that takes satellites over the poles of the Earth.

porous   A substance such as a rock with lots of tiny holes in it is porous.

predator   An animal that hunts other animals.

prey   Animals that are hunted and eaten by predators.

primary colour   One of the three colours of light that humans can see – green, red or blue.

producer   A plant, that produces its own food by photosynthesis.

proteins   Nutrients found in foods such as fish, used in your body for growth and repair.

pupil   The gap in the iris of the eye that lets light in.

quadrat   A wooden frame measuring one metre on all four sides.

radioactive   Radioactive atoms are unstable and break down, producing large amounts of energy.

random samples   Taking samples from different places without choosing the places deliberately.

ratio   A way of showing a scale factor. For example, a scale of 1:10 means you have to multiply your number or measurement by 10 to get the real measurement.

ray   A thin beam of light.

recommended daily intakes (RDI) and recommended daily allowances (RDA)   Levels set by the Government that advise about the amounts of different nutrients eaten each day.

red blood cells   Special cells that carry oxygen around in your blood.

reflected   When light or sound bounces off a surface, it is reflected.

refraction   Bending of light when it travels from one material to another.

relaxing   When a muscle stops contracting and can be pulled back to its normal length, we say it is relaxing.

renewable   An energy resource that is replaced as we use it is renewable.

reproduce   To make more organisms of the same species.

reproductive system   An organ system that is involved in reproduction.

respiration   The process by which plants and animals break down their food to release the chemical energy from it.

respiratory system   An organ system that takes oxygen into the blood and gets rid of carbon dioxide.

rickets   A disease caused by not eating enough vitamin D in the diet, in which the bones are soft.

rock cycle   A cycle that describes how the three rock types change from one to another over millions of years.

root   A plant organ that takes in water and minerals, and anchors the plant in the soil.

root hair cells   Special cells found in roots that are adapted to absorb water.

roughage   Another name for fibre in the diet.

salt   A substance formed in a neutralisation reaction.

sample   A small part of something, used to represent the whole.

sandstone   A type of sedimentary rock made up of grains of sand.

satellite   An object that orbits a larger object.

scattered   When light is reflected in many directions by a rough surface, it is scattered.

scrubbers   Devices that remove polluting gases such as sulfur dioxide from the fumes given out by power stations.

scurvy   A disease caused by not eating enough vitamin C in the diet, in which the gums bleed and the skin does not heal.

seasons   Times of different climate during the year. In the UK we have four seasons – spring, summer, autumn and winter.

secondary colour One of the three colours of light produced by mixing two primary colours.

sediment Small pieces of rock and dead living things which build up in layers at the bottoms of lakes or seas over millions of years.

sedimentary rock A type of rock made up from layers of sediment that have built up over millions of years and become cemented together.

seeds Structures used for reproduction in flowering plants and conifers.

shadow Darkness due to an object blocking the light.

shale A type of sedimentary rock formed from clay.

shutter Something used to close an opening to stop the light coming through.

skeletal system An organ system made up of bones. It protects and supports your body and allows you to move.

skeleton Another word for the skeletal system.

slate A type of metamorphic rock that has a layered structure.

small intestine The part of the gut where enzymes and bile are added in alkaline conditions to digest the different substances in food. Absorption also happens here.

sodium A metallic element. A sodium salt is formed when sodium hydroxide neutralises an acid.

soil A mixture of mineral grains made when rocks are broken up on the Earth's surface.

solar cell A device that takes in light energy and gives out electrical energy.

solar eclipse An eclipse that occurs when the Moon blocks the Sun's light from reaching the Earth. A shadow passes across the Earth.

solar energy Energy given out by the Sun.

solar furnace A device that concentrates thermal energy from the Sun and uses the thermal energy to heat a material.

Solar System The Sun and the objects orbiting it, including Earth and the other planets.

solubility A measure of how much of a solute will dissolve at a particular temperature.

source Where something starts or is produced.

specialised A cell that is adapted to carry out a particular function is specialised.

spectrum The colours in white light – red, orange, yellow, green, blue, indigo, violet.

spores Structures used for reproduction in mosses and ferns.

stem A plant organ that holds the plant up and transports water and sugars.

stomach The part of the gut where the food is churned up and mixed with enzymes in acidic conditions.

summer solstice The longest day, on 21 June in the UK.

tendon A tissue that joins muscles to bones.

thermal energy   Heat energy – the energy given out by a hot object.

tides   The movement of water produced by the gravitational pull of the Moon. Tides can be used as an energy resource.

tissue   A group of similar cells that carry out the same job.

topsoil   The top layer of soil, made of tiny grains of rock and humus.

total eclipse   An eclipse viewed from a place where the shadow is complete.

toxic   Toxic means poisonous. Substances that may cause serious health risks and even death if inhaled, taken internally or absorbed through the skin are toxic.

toxic waste   Waste that contains poisonous substances.

translucent   A material that allows some light to pass through is translucent.

transparent   A material that allows light to pass through is transparent.

transported   Moved to another place. Pieces of weathered rock may be transported by wind, glaciers or water.

turbine   A device for changing movement in one direction into a spinning movement.

universal indicator   An indicator that has a range of colours showing the strength of acidity or alkalinity on the pH scale.

vein   In animals – a blood vessel in which blood flows back to the heart. In plants – a tube-like structure that carries water, mineral salts and food around the plant.

villi (singular villus)   Finger-like structures in the small intestine which increase the area for the absorption of digested food.

vitamin   A substance such as vitamin C that is needed in the diet in very small amounts to keep your body healthy.

vitamin A   A vitamin found in carrots that keeps your skin and eyes healthy.

vitamin C   A vitamin found in fresh fruit and vegetables.

vitamin D   A vitamin found in milk and butter and made in your body in sunlight, which gives you strong bones and teeth.

water   A compound of hydrogen and oxygen. Water is the solvent in which all the chemical reactions in your body take place.

wave energy   The kinetic (movement) energy of waves.

weathering   Breaking rock down by chemical or physical processes.

wind energy   The kinetic (movement) energy of the wind.

wind turbine   A device that takes in the kinetic (movement) energy of the wind and gives out electrical energy.

winter solstice   The shortest day, on 21 December in the UK.

year   The time taken for the Earth to orbit the Sun.

yellow   A colour of light produced by mixing red and green light.

Note: page numbers in **bold** show where a word is **explained** in the text. There are also definitions in the Glossary on pages **136–45**.

Photo acknowledgments

The authors and publishers would like to thank the following for permission to use photographs:

Cover photos: Ostriches, Tony Stone Images. **Colourful Windmill**, Science Photo Library/Martin Bond. **Volcanic Eruption**, Oxford Scientific Film/Hjalmar R. Bardarson.

1.1d, **1.2b**, **1.2c**, Andrew Lambert. **1.3a 1–7**, **1.4a**, **1.4b**, Andrew Lambert. **1.4d**, Garden & Wildlife Matters. **1.5a**, Peter Gould. **1.5e**, **1.6a**, **1.6b**, **1.7b**, Andrew Lambert. **1.7c**, Environmental Images/John Morrison. **1.7e**, Andrew Lambert. **1.7g**, SPL/Simon Fraser. **2.1b**, Popperfoto. **2.1c**, Tony Stone/Manoj Shah (Pigs) Robert Harding. **2.2d**, **2.2e**, Corbis. **2.3a**, SPL. **2.4a**, SPL/John Daugherty. **2.4b**, SPL (knuckle – D. Roberts) **2.4e**, SPL/Clinical Radiology Dept. Salisbury District Hospital. **2.5a**, SPL/Quest. **2.5e**, Action Plus (Glyn Kirk, Neil Tingle). **3.1b**, SPL/PLI. **3.1c**, SPL/Novosti. **3.1e**, SPL/NASA. **3.2b** SPL/Space Telescope Institute, NASA, NASA coloured by Mehau Kuluk, US Geological Survey, NASA, Space Telescope Science, Institute/NASA, NASA, NASA, NASA, NASA. **3.3a**, SPL/Jerry Mason, Andrew McClenaghan, Amy Trustram Eve. **3.3b**, SPL/Pekka Parviainen. **3.3c**, SPL/Space Telescope Institute/NASA. **3.4b**, **3.4c**, SPL. **3.4d**, SPL/Dr Jeremy Burgess. **3.4e**, Mary Evans Picture Library. **3.5b**, SPL/Dr Fred Espenak. **3.7c**, **3.7e**, SPL/European Space Agency. **4.1b**, SPL/Sheila Terry. **4.1g**, IBM Corporation, Research Division, Almaden Research Centre. **4.2a**, Andrew Lambert **4.4a**, **4.4b**, **4.4c**, **4.4g**, Andrew Lambert. **4.4i**, Robert Harding. **4.5a**, Andrew Lambert. **4.5d**, SPL/David Nunuk. **4.6a** Tony Stone Images/Randy Wells. **4.6d**, **4.7a**, **4.7c**, Andrew Lambert. **4.8c**, Peter Gould. **4.8d**, Barnaby's Picture Library. **4.8e**, **4.8f**, Andrew Lambert. **5.1a**, Tony Stone/Mark Segal. **5.1b**, Holt Studios/Phillip Mitchell. **5.1c**, **5.1d**, Holt Studios/Nigel Cattlin. **5.2a**, **5.2b**, **5.2c**, **5.2d**, Andrew Lambert. **5.3c**, The Stock Market, Robert Harding. **5.3e**, SPL/Oscar Burriel. **5.3f**, Action-Plus/Glyn Kirk. **5.4d**, SPL/Eye of Science, Juergen Berger, Max-Planck Institute. **6.1d**, Andrew Lambert. **6.1f**, Tony Stone/Yvette Cardozo. **6.1g**, Tony Stone/Lorne Resnick. **6.1l**, Action-plus/Andy Willsheer. **6.1m**, Popperfoto. **6.1n**, **6.1o**, SPL/NASA. **6.2a**, Andrew Lambert. **6.3d**, Environmental Images/Matt Sampson. **6.4a**, Environmental Images. **6.5a**, Holt Studios/Nigel Cattlin. **6.5b**, Environmental Images/David Hoffman. **6.6b**, Tony Stone/Robert Cameron. **6.6d**, Environmental Images/John Novis. **6.7a**, Fiat. **6.7d**, Associated Press/Steve Holland. **7.1a**, **7.1b**, Natural History Museum, London. **7.1c**, **7.2a**, **7.2c**, GSF Picture Gallery. **7.2e**, S Nicholson. **7.2f**, Environmental Images/Trevor Perry. **7.3a**, GSF Picture Library/Robert Harding/Roy Rainford. **7.3b**, Andrew Lambert. **7.4a**, GSF Picture Library. **7.4b**, Environmental Images/Clive Jones. **7.4c**, **7.4d**, **7.5b**, **7.5c**, **7.5d**, **7.6a**, **7.6b**, **7.6c**, **7.6d**, **7.6e**, **7.7c**, **7.7d**, **7.7e**, GSF Picture Library. **8.1a**, News Team International/Mike Sharp. **8.1c**, Garden & Wildlife Matters. **8.1d**, Robert Harding/Adam Woolfitt. **8.2a**, SPL/Simon Fraser. **8.2b**, Wildlife Matters. **8.2c**, Garden Matters/Steffie Shields. **8.2d**, SPL/Simon Fraser/Eye of Science. **8.2e**, SPL/Simon Fraser/Claude Nuridsany & Marie Perennou. **8.2f**, SPL/Alex Bartel/John Howard. **8.3a**, **8.3c**, Garden & Wildlife Matters. **8.5a**, Oxford Scientific Films/David & Sue Cayless. **8.7c**, **8.7b**, Andrew Lambert. **9.1c**, SPL/Martin Dohrn. **9.2b**, Andrew Lambert. **9.3f**, SPL/David Scharf. **9.3g**, Trevor Hill. **9.4a**, **9.4b**, **9.4f**, Andrew Lambert. **9.4j**, Bruce Coleman Collection/Kim Taylor. **9.5a**, SPL/David Parker. **9.5b**, SPL/ Pekka Parviainen. **9.5d**, Robert Harding/Tim Hall. **9.5e**, SPL/Adrienne Hart-Davis. **9.6a**, SPL/Vaughn Fleming. **9.7a**, Andrew Lambert. **9.7c**, Redferns/Nicky J Sims. **9.7e**, Redferns/David Redfern. **9.8a**, SPL/Kent Wood.

The publishers have made every effort to trace copyright holders, but if they have inadvertently overlooked any, they will be pleased to make the necessary arrangements at the first opportunity.

154